THE SAVVY WRITER'S GUIDE TO PRODUCTIVITY

HOW TO WORK LESS, FINISH WRITING YOUR STORY OR BOOK, AND FIND THE SUCCESS YOU DESERVE

BRYAN COLLINS

BECOME A *Writer* TODAY

PREFACE

This book uses British English.
Thank you for supporting this work.

CONTENTS

GET YOUR EXCLUSIVE BONUS

Before you start reading, I've created a **FREE video master class**. You'll cut months off how long it takes you to write your book by using my best tactics and strategies.

WAIT!

DID YOU CLAIM YOUR FREE BONUS?

VISIT
becomeawritertoday.com/author

If you want to get this masterclass today, please visit http://becomeawritertoday.com/author

INTRODUCTION

Writing is hard work.

You've got to think of an idea. Shape it into something usable. Write it. Rewrite it. Edit it. And then rewrite it again. It's mentally and physically demanding, and many writers give up before they finish.

Perhaps you find it difficult to take an idea from concept to completion.

Maybe you struggle to produce anything meaningful from a few hours of writing each week.

Possibly do you just want to create a habit of writing every day?

Take a deep breath.

It's OK.

You're not alone.

If you opened up this book, you're ready to become a different kind of writer.

Any aspiring writer can learn how to finish their work. You don't need to be a genius, possess divine gift, or have the discipline of a Zen monk to finish a writing an article or a book.

So, don't feel intimidated by the blank page.

You can cultivate your ability to become more productive by showing up in front of that blank page and cultivating your craft every day.

I've spent years working as a journalist, copywriter and blogger. I've made a lot of mistakes–some public, some private–and learnt many hard lessons about what productive, successful writers do.

I've studied and written about popular productivity methods on my blog *Become a Writer Today*. I've also read hundreds of articles and books about writing.

I'm going to share 33 simple but effective productivity strategies for any writer who wants to finish what they started and become more successful.

WHAT YOU'LL DISCOVER IN THIS BOOK

Why 33 productivity strategies?

I started this book by writing 101 writing strategies through studying how literary heavyweights and renowned non-fiction writers approach their craft.

I also spent time studying the methodology behind popular productivity techniques that business people use to accomplish more in their personal and professional lives.

I wanted to find that point where business and the arts intersect, and in this book, I regularly reference authors we can learn from.

But I'm not going to lie to you.

I almost gave up writing this book–twice, but starting with a goal of writing 101 strategies made the job of writing 33 strategies feel achievable.

Think of the marathon runner who has to run 26 miles— the first 13 are easy; it's the second 13 that present the real problems.

So once I had 101 strategies, I took Ernest Hemingway's advice.

He said, "The first draft of everything is shit."

Authors like Hemingway can teach the rest of us how to achieve anything with words, ideas and a blank page.

I worked through each of the 101 strategies and discarded what wasn't working. This kind of brutal editing is a process every productive writer becomes intimately familiar with.

Then I refined my research and ideas into 33 strategies that will help you get to the end of whatever you're writing.

What I've just described–the strategy of generating more ideas by setting the bar higher–forms part of one of the 33 strategies you'll learn about in this book.

HOW TO USE THIS BOOK

You can use the 33 strategies to consistently publish on your blog, finally finish writing your book, and balance writing with the rest of your life.

To help you get out of your creative jams, I've included proven writing prompts you can use to kick-start your writing projects.

I wrote each of these strategies as stand-alone chapters with steps you can put into practice today. Although there's a natural order to this book, you can dip in and out of each strategy and apply it to whatever you're writing.

You can read this book from start to finish, use it as a companion guide or apply the individual strategies most relevant to how you like to work or write. This book isn't specifically about fiction or non-fiction writing, but I reference both kinds of creative work.

Whatever your interests, I hope this book helps you become a more confident and successful writer.

Using these 33 strategies, you'll be able to write every day, create a writing habit that sticks and finish what you started.

You will become *the productive writer*.

LEAVE YOUR INTRODUCTION
TILL LAST

L et me tell you a secret.

Productive writers create their introduction last.

The purpose of the first sentence is to convince a reader to continue to the second sentence. The purpose of the first paragraph is to convince the reader to continue to the second. The purpose of the first chapter...and so on.

Think about it: What's the first thing a customer in a bookshop looks at when they open a new book? Unless you're one of those crazy types who likes to read the ending, it's the first line.

Almost every writer I've met writes their first paragraph and their first sentence last.

No matter if you're writing a book, article, blog post or copy for a webpage, you must capture and hold the reader's attention, which is a valuable commodity.

Writing a solid first line or a good opening is hard work. If you don't know what the subsequent sentences, paragraphs and chapters are about, writing a great opening is impossible.

During your next writing project, don't worry about the

beginning until you reach the end. Then read through your work and summarise it in a sentence or two. If you can come up with a good hook or metaphor to draw the reader in, even better.

Once you're happy with your introduction, reread your conclusion and explore how you can link the two together.

Perhaps you have an idea or a metaphor you can return to.

Maybe you can use similar language to answer a question you raised in the introduction.

A book's introduction and conclusion are like sign-posts. They let the reader know what lies ahead and where he or she just visited.

Whatever your approach, work hard on your opening and even harder on your first line. Smooth, buff, polish and make it shine. The reader should find your opening line irresistible.

Your first line can and should make the reader feel inspired, curious or motivated for your next line.

Whatever you do, don't bore them with a long, ponderous sentence. Make your reader feel something, and they'll keep reading.

Whenever I'm struggling to find an opening, I go back and read great first lines for inspiration.

With this in mind, here are ten of my favourite opening lines of all time. Each of these succeed because they make the reader feel something.

- "Call me Ishmael." – Herman Melville, *Moby-Dick* (1851)
- "It was a bright cold day in April, and the clocks were striking thirteen." – George Orwell, *1984* (1949)
- "It was the best of times, it was the worst of times,

it was the age of wisdom, it was the age of foolishness, it was the epoch of belief, it was the epoch of incredulity, it was the season of Light, it was the season of Darkness, it was the spring of hope, it was the winter of despair." – Charles Dickens, *A Tale of Two Cities* (1859)

- "Lolita, light of my life, fire of my loins." – Vladimir Nabokov, *Lolita* (1955)

- "Happy families are all alike; every unhappy family is unhappy in its own way." – Leo Tolstoy, *Anna Karenina* (1877)

- "It is a truth universally acknowledged, that a single man in possession of a good fortune, must be in want of a wife." – Jane Austen, *Pride and Prejudice* (1813)

- "It was a queer, sultry summer, the summer they electrocuted the Rosenbergs, and I didn't know what I was doing in New York." – Sylvia Plath, *The Bell Jar* (1963)

- "If you really want to hear about it, the first thing you'll probably want to know is where I was born, and what my lousy childhood was like, and how my parents were occupied and all before they had me, and all that David Copperfield kind of crap, but I don't feel like going into it, if you want to know the truth." – J.D. Salinger, *The Catcher In The Rye* (1951)

- "In my younger and more vulnerable years my father gave me some advice that I've been turning over in my mind ever since. Whenever you feel like criticising anyone, he told me, just remember that all the people in this world haven't had the advantages that you've had." – F. Scott Fitzgerald, *The Great Gatsby* (1925)

- "As Gregor Samsa awoke one morning from uneasy dreams he found himself transformed in his bed into a monstrous vermin." – Franz Kafka, *The Metamorphosis* (1915)

HOW TO USE THE INVERTED PYRAMID

Journalists use the inverted pyramid to arrange the key facts of what they are writing.

This concept came about because editors and printers of early newspapers sometimes didn't have enough print space to fit entire stories into their papers.

They needed a way of removing information quickly to make the text of each story fit, and cutting off the bottom paragraphs of news stories was the fastest way to do this.

So journalists started writing the most important point first, the second most important point second, and so on.

Although printing technology has improved, the inverted pyramid still applies because newspaper readers don't always read a story all the way through.

A reader will glance at a headline, and if it's of interest they'll pick up the paper and read the rest of the story.

Today, journalists use the headline, the first sentence, and the first paragraph to answer the following questions in increasing levels of detail:

- What happened?
- When did it happen?
- To whom did it happen?
- Where did it happen?
- How did it happen?
- Why did it happen?

Writers also use the inverted pyramid for web pages

because the average visitor doesn't stay for more than 10 to 20 seconds on a webpage.

So an online writer has to capture the reader's attention by putting the most important information first and writing for people who scan digital copy.

The inverted pyramid works for short, non-fiction writing projects. You can apply it to newsletters, social media posts, copy for web pages, blog posts or articles.

If you are writing for the web, you can use the inverted pyramid to get to the point faster. Say what is most important first and induce the reader to stay a little longer.

The inverted pyramid isn't as effective when your writing has more room to breathe and when you can count on the reader's attention for a thesis or an article of more than 3,000 words, for example.

Then you have the time and space to expand on your arguments or tell a story.

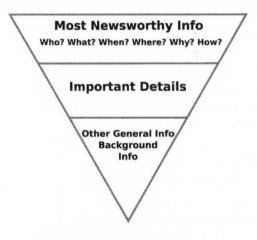

The Inverted Pyramid, via Wikimedia and The Air Force Departmental Publishing Office (AFDPO, 2011)

OPEN WITH FLAIR

The introduction is the hardest part of any article or story to write. If you're struggling to create a compelling opening, leave it till last. When you're finished writing, you'll have a better idea of how to begin.

If you're still stuck, open like a journalist. They write their articles with the end in mind. Journalists know what their news story is about and understand what they're saying before they start writing.

A journalist doesn't begin a news article hoping by the time they reach the last paragraph they will have said something important or newsworthy.

Neither does the productive writer.

WARM UP LIKE A PRO

"If you want to be the best, you have to do things that other people aren't willing to do." – Michael Phelps

Do you warm up before you write?

The Olympic swimmer Michael Phelps begins exercising in a pool separate to the competition for 45 minutes before a big race.

The world's fastest man, Usain Bolt, practices sprinting near the track before he competes. And tennis champion Roger Federer skips, jumps and stretches before a match.

Writers who want to become more productive should apply the same approach to their craft.

It takes five or 10 minutes of writing to forget the distractions of the day, warm up and pay attention to whatever you're supposed to be working on. These first few minutes of writing might not produce anything of merit.

The first few minutes of any writing session should help you focus on the task ahead.

Warming up will help you overcome procrastination. If

you do it regularly, those first few minutes of writing will feel less painful.

You can warm up in many different ways before you write.

Reading poetry or listening to music can fire up the left side of your brain for more creative work. Reading a passage from a book or an article can engage your critical faculties for non-fiction writing.

Printing out, reading and annotating the entirety of the previous day's work is also useful if you're about to embark on an editing session.

You can use a writing prompt to warm up today too.

JUMP-START YOUR WRITING

These writing prompts aren't meant as final first lines for your work.

Instead, you can use them as a jumping-off point into your work or for freewriting.

Take one of these lines, write it down and then freewrite whatever comes to mind for at least 30 minutes. I suggest using a kitchen timer.

This is long enough to accomplish something on the blank page but not so long that it feels overwhelming.

Later when you've written something more polished, go back and delete the writing prompt.

If you dislike my selection of prompts, take a great first line from your favourite book, poem or story and use that.

Whatever your choice, writing prompts will help you stand on the shoulders of giants. And up there, you can see for miles.

- "I remember the last time I…"
- "I remember the first time I…"

- "The next time I…"
- "It tasted like…"
- "It felt like…"
- "It sounded like…"
- "We were wrong about…"
- "We were right about…"
- "That was the day we…"
- "This is our new…"
- "It's here."
- "I learnt that…"
- "I made a terrible mistake when…"
- "Nobody expected us to…"
- "Do you know why…"
- "It's always important to…"
- "Most people don't know this but…"
- "I probably shouldn't be telling you this, but…"
- "Here's a secret nobody knows…"
- "I do this because…"
- "Admit it."
- "I found out that…"
- "He gave us a…"
- "She took a…"
- "We found a…"
- "I was in pain."
- "We discovered…"
- "Today is a good day for…"
- "Tomorrow is a bad day for…"
- "This time it will be different."
- "We need to talk about…"
- "You need to face up to…"
- "Our only hope is…"
- "On my desk I can see…"
- "Outside the window…"
- "I ate…"

- "If I was…"
- "When I'm…"
- "Go to…"
- "Now that we…"
- "We argued about…"
- "Being wrong is hard because…"
- "Being right is lonely because…"
- "Together we can…"
- "Apart we are…"
- "Let me guess."
- "If I understand you correctly, you think…"
- "My friend is…"
- "I love her because…"
- "I hate him because…"
- "We're going to…"
- "Let's take a trip to…"
- "My favourite…"
- "I'm lost."
- "We want to get to…"
- "The weather is…"
- "We're going to eat…"
- "Food is…"
- "Water is…"
- "Money is…"
- "Help is…"
- "Sex is…"
- "Last night I dreamt of…"
- "I slept for…"
- "I'm working for…"
- "I failed at…"
- "I succeeded at…"
- "You showed me how to…"
- "He explained that…"
- "She made us laugh when…"

- "My hero is…"
- "My enemy is…"
- "I regret…"
- "This time we went too far."
- "I told him…"
- "She told me…"
- "I looked in the mirror and saw…"
- "Black."
- "White."
- "I awoke at 3:00 a.m. and realised…"
- "I should have listened."
- "He won't do that again."
- "It was the first storm of the year…"
- "Her eyes are…"
- "His hands make me want to…"
- "She tastes like…"
- "He feels like…"
- "Danger."
- "How can we…"
- "Open your…"
- "Keep it safe."
- "It's a new day."
- "It's later than we think."
- "If I ever see another…"
- "The best day of my life was…"
- "The worst day of my life was…"
- "When I'm king…"
- "You could be a queen of…"
- "Looking back…"
- "They caught me."
- "I was crushed because…"

If need more help with writing prompts, check out *Yes, You Can Write! 101 Proven Writing Prompts that Will Help You*

Find Creative Ideas Faster for Your Journal, Blogging, Writing Your Book and More.

In this short free book, I provide different detailed prompts for many kinds of writing and elaborate on how to create personal prompts.

HOW TO FREEWRITE

Freewriting is simple to learn, and every productive writer should have this skill in their toolbox.

All you have to do is sit at your desk and write about anything that comes to mind without interruption for five, 10 or 20 minutes. If you write nothing but gibberish, whatever you do, don't stop writing.

When you freewrite, you're not trying to accomplish or complete anything on the blank page.

Author Mark Levy wrote in his book *Accidental Genius*,

Freewriting...pushes the brain to think longer, deeper and more unconventionally than it normally would.

Freewriting can help you clear mental blocks, come up with better ideas, write more honestly, think differently from your peers, and find a new perspective for your writing.

You can freewrite a cover letter for a job application, copy for your website, a blog post, a magazine article or a chapter for your book.

If you want to try freewriting as a warm-up exercise for your current writing project, don't worry about capturing fully formed ideas.

Instead, just type or write about anything that comes to mind.

It's OK if you jump from one idea to the next. Document

your thoughts as they arise without holding back. Don't edit or censure yourself.

If something daft comes, like the sound of a dog on the street, write that down too. And if someone interrupts your train of thought, record that you were interrupted.

If you keep freewriting, you will overtake your brain's ability to edit, and you'll break past your internal critic.

You will reach a place where you can write about wild ideas and make connections that otherwise wouldn't have been possible if you'd held back.

Your word count will shoot up, sure. And if most of what you write is rubbish, at the end of your freewriting session, you can extract one or two good ideas and then spend time developing these into something more usable for your current writing project.

WRITE WITHOUT EDITING YOURSELF

Freewriting works only if you don't question or criticise every sentence, idea and story you put down on the blank page.

Instead, let the words flow freely through your fingers onto the page without pausing or questioning what you're writing.

Then when you've finished your freewriting for the day, spend time polishing, buffing and making your prose shine.

WRITE WHATEVER COMES TO MIND

Freewriting enables you to follow a train of thought in new and exciting directions.

When you're freewriting, record what you're thinking or if you feel distracted. It doesn't matter if it's unrelated to the topic you're writing about. This could mean recording the the colour of a plant on your desk or a swear word.

Don't hold back.

TIME YOUR FREEWRITING SESSIONS

Get a clock or open the timer on your computer. Set it for 25 minutes and write. When the buzzer sounds, take a short break and repeat. Do this two to four times before taking a longer break.

FREEWRITE FOR AN HOUR OR LONGER

If you're struggling to make a breakthrough, freewrite for an extended period without taking a break.

Yes, this is mentally and physically demanding, but you don't have to do it very often. It will help you overcome those difficult barriers every writer faces at some point.

KEEP YOUR HAND MOVING

This tip is straight from the pages of Natalie Goldberg's excellent book *Writing Down the Bones: Freeing the Writer Within*.

An advocate of freewriting, or "writing practice" as she calls it, Goldberg recommends "keeping your hand moving."

If you're a typist, don't take your fingers from the keys until you've finished writing.

If you prefer a pen, this means keeping the pen pressed between your fingers. And if you like to dictate your writing, keep the dictation machine recording until you're done.

KEEP A LIST OF TOPICS

I use Evernote to organise my writing. Inside, I keep a notebook full of topics that I want to freewrite about.

Examples include ideas for short stories, sentence fragments, blog posts, and ideas that I want to expand on.

Then, when I want to freewrite, I pick one item from my notebook and go with it. Keeping these kinds of lists means I spend less time looking for a topic and more time freewriting.

USE OTHER WRITING TECHNIQUES

Freewriting is just one writing technique you can employ to advance your work.

Sometimes, it makes more sense to plan your writing in advance or to aim towards a target word count.

Combining freewriting with other kinds of writing sessions such as editing, outlining chapters etc. It will help you mix things up during the week, test your boundaries and avoid becoming bored with the process.

KEEP YOUR CAST-OFFS

Freewriting produces a lot of leftover ideas that don't immediately belong anywhere. Don't throw this writing in the bin or delete it.

Instead, keep your cast-offs in your journal or a file on your computer.

A time will come when it makes sense to return to your leftovers and extract something useful. These leftovers also serve as markers for your progress as a writer.

Don't worry though. I address how to do this more in chapter four.

EXPAND ON IDEA

I read a lot of non-fiction books, and I regularly come across ideas that surprise, inspire or confound me.

Sometimes I take these ideas and expand on them during freewriting sessions. Freewriting about ideas helps me internalise them and figure out how I can use them.

If you want to do the same, underline key passages in the books you're reading, write notes in the margins and review these when you've finished reading The Kindle is ideal for this.

Then pick one or two ideas and use them as topics for your next freewriting session.

FREEWRITE A PROBLEM UPSIDE DOWN

Are you having trouble with a particularly difficult writing project?

Perhaps the feedback from a client wasn't helpful.

Or maybe you can't figure out the right arc for your story.

Write down this problem at the top of your page.

Then freewrite everything about the problem that's bothering you and what you're afraid of. Freewrite all the solutions you can think of.

If you get lucky, you'll make a breakthrough. If you don't, you're still venting your frustrations and practice writing at the same time.

Think of it as therapy and writing practice rolled into one.

WHY YOU SHOULD FREEWRITE FOR FUN

Sometimes you need to hit a word count, and press publish.

Other times, writing is supposed to be fun, you need to try something different or go in a new direction.

For the latter, freewriting is the perfect writing technique. This week, allocate 30 minutes of time for freewriting. Use it to write about whatever you want. It's your guilty pleasure.

Are you still unsure about freewriting? Why not freewrite about the ways it can help you finish what you started? Who knows where you'll end up?

STOP WAITING FOR INSPIRATION
(IT'S NOT COMING)

"Don't be daunted. Just do your job. Continue to show up for your piece of it, whatever that might be." – Elizabeth Gilbert

What would happen if a professional athlete stopped training for an event because they were tired of their sport?

If he or she made a habit of not training, they'd lose their next event.

What would happen if an engineer stopped working on a construction project because he didn't feel excited about plans for the project?

He'd lose his job.

What happens to the writer who waits for inspiration to arrive?

She doesn't write at all.

Writing is hard work. It's demanding and time-consuming, and it requires you to sit in one place and concentrate for extended periods of time. If you want to write professionally, treat the work seriously.

Like any profession, it's your job to turn up in front of the blank page each day and not just when inspiration arrives. It's your duty to write when you don't feel like writing, when you're tired, angry, anxious or afraid.

Leave divine moments of inspiration for the creative geniuses.

American short story writer and author John Updike wasn't one for waiting around for inspiration. He wrote for several hours each day.

Updike published his first work, a collection of poetry called *The Carpentered Hen,* in 1958. Thereafter, he published a book almost every year.

"I've never believed that one should wait until one is inspired, because I think that the pleasures of not writing are so great that if you ever start indulging them, you'll never write again," he said.

Stop waiting around for an idea or solution to whatever causes you problems. Force yourself into the chair and start to write.

The first few sentences might not make much sense, but several sentences in you'll realise you're not as tired or devoid of ideas as you thought; you were just procrastinating.

Even if you turn up and produce nothing of value, at least you put in a morning or an evening's work. Take heart from author and speaker Elizabeth Gilbert. She said,

> Creativity itself doesn't care at all about results - the only thing it craves is the process. Learn to love the process and let whatever happens next happen, without fussing too much about it. Work like a monk, or a mule, or some other representative metaphor for diligence. Love the work. Destiny will do what it wants with you, regardless.

ACCEPT YOUR SUBCONSCIOUS

The subconscious is a powerful beast.

It needs food and attention.

Take notes, turn up every day in front of the blank page and make a concerted effort to finish what you're working on. The writer who does this understands how important it is to feed his or her inner beast.

If you write sales copy, your subconscious is hungry for the words that sell, for words written by talented copy-writers.

If you write articles for magazines, your subconscious is waiting for exotic, fresh and colourful stories.

If you write blog posts, the subconscious wants to devour in-depth, meaningful posts so it can present you with new ideas.

If you write fiction, your subconscious craves anecdotes, stories, characters and dialogue.

Keeping the beast happy also means giving it time and space to roam free through your mind.

I'm talking about daydreaming.

Most creative people are familiar with those small eureka moments of life whereby a solution suddenly presents itself when you're working on something else entirely. These ideas can turn up when you're in the shower, eating a meal, watching television or out for a walk.

Of course, it would be more convenient if we could summon these ideas at will in front of the blank page, but the subconscious is a wild animal; it can't be tamed.

French artist Henri Matisse gave his subconscious time and space while painting landscapes. He sometimes stopped working to meditate on the environment around him. He did this at length before returning to his canvas with a new perspective.

Matisse did pretty well for himself in the end. As one of the greatest and most productive painters of the twentieth century, he finished several dozen masterpieces during his lifetime. So, don't be afraid to pause what you are doing.

Let the beast run free.

LEARN FROM ALBERT EINSTEIN

Are you still procrastinating?

Do you need just a little bit more encouragement to pick up the pen?

Are you still thinking, "But I could accomplish more if I didn't have to do all these other things?"

Take some productivity lessons from Albert Einstein.

He is one of the most famous scientific writers of all time. Although he is more famous for his mathematical equations than his writing, Einstein's life shows writers can succeed because of life's day-to-day struggles and not in spite of them.

Einstein's Peers Rejected Him

During his early twenties, Einstein spent several years seeking employment as a teaching assistant. He struggled to find meaningful work, and he couldn't get his dissertation published as part of an application for a doctorate.

Einstein even sent professors copies of his dissertation with a postage-paid card, to encourage them to reply and offer feedback (sometimes we take email for granted!).

Numerous leading professors and employers in Germany, Austria, Italy and Switzerland rejected Einstein repeatedly. At one stage, Einstein became so despondent about his career that he contemplated abandoning science for engineering.

His father, an engineer, wrote to Wilhelm Ostwald, the Professor of Chemistry of Leipzig, and implored Ostwald to read Einstein's paper and write a few words of encouragement.

Ostwald didn't reply (although much later he did nominate Einstein for the Nobel Prize).

Later Einstein published a series of landmark papers that overturned the basics of physics, but he spent several more years waiting for the academic and professional recognition he deserved.

Today, writers have much more opportunities than Einstein to make their voices heard. If a gatekeeper refuses our work, we can use a blog to build a platform, enter contests or self-publish a book.

Today, it doesn't take a genius to find an audience.

Einstein Pursued Many Interests

Einstein loved music since he was a child, and he became an accomplished violinist. He often entertained dinner party guests, academics, friends and his family by playing Mozart.

He didn't care much for material possessions or appearances, but he did bring his violin almost everywhere.

Einstein once played with noted Russian violinist Toscha Seidel and afterwards explained his theory of relativity to Seidel.

He stopped playing later in life only when his fingers struggled with the violin strings.

Einstein's first love was science, but he still made time for other passions and interests. Writers don't have to pursue their craft at all costs; if anything, your writing will improve if you make time for other passions.

Einstein Challenged Himself

Einstein saw himself as a nonconformist and a rebel. This belief system was both a result of the times he lived in and his personal character.

Einstein lived through two World Wars, and he had to leave Hitler's Germany for America because he was Jewish.

As a younger man, he suggested academic life wasn't conducive to great work, and according to his biographer Walter Isaacson, he took delight in challenging the prevailing wisdom of his academic peers.

From the 1920s onwards, many of Einstein's theories were challenged or overturned by a new branch of physics: quantum mechanics. This branch of physics described randomness in nature, but Einstein dismissed it saying, "God does not play dice."

He spent the later part of his life researching a way of unifying his general theory of relativism with electro-magnetism.

Einstein's contemporaries, who were more concerned with quantum mechanics, regarded his quest as rather quaint and even as a waste of Einstein's time.

Einstein didn't care.

Always the rebel, he felt he'd achieved enough status and security in life to spend time researching areas of physics that his younger peers would have been discredited for.

For Einstein, pursuing a passion was more important than what others thought of him or how he spent his time.

Don't seek success for its own sake. It's more important that you challenge yourself, publish your work and avoid complacency.

He Didn't Regard His Craft as Work

In 1955, a 76-year-old Einstein died in hospital from a longstanding stomach ailment.

On his deathbed, he left 12 sets of equations that formed parts of Einstein's search for a unified field theory. He also left an undelivered speech, which he had just written for Israel Independence Day.

I'm not suggesting writing on your deathbed, but Einstein's story demonstrates a life's work can take on a greater meaning if we're passionate enough about our craft.

At the very least, remember Einstein's advice for scientists and by extension writers, "If you can't explain it simply, you don't understand it well enough."

FAIL LIKE A GENIUS

Genius or not, Einstein had many personal flaws.

Einstein married Marić Mileva in 1903, and he divorced her in 1919 after a difficult and unhappy marriage. He also rarely saw his son Eduard Tete, who had schizophrenia and had a more difficult life in various mental health institutions.

Einstein married his second wife Elsa Löwenthal in 1919 and, although they were married until her death in 1936, he had several affairs.

After Elsa's death, Einstein praised a friend for managing to live in harmony with a woman, saying this was one thing he failed at.

He could also be cold and distant. As a younger man, he often made life harder for himself by deliberately antagonising and challenging his peers.

Einstein overcame many personal and professional obstacles, but he also failed and failed often. He experienced the same pain and suffering many of us go through.

FUEL UP ON IDEAS

"The knowledge of all things is possible." – Leonardo da Vinci

You can't drive a car without fuel, and you can't write if you haven't got any ideas.

The good news is that unlike fuel, ideas are everywhere. All you have to do is get into the habit of regularly filling up your creative tank, and you will always have what you need to write.

This creative habit is one accomplished writers, artists and even inventors cultivate.

When Leonardo da Vinci died in 1519, he left behind dozens of notebooks filled with ideas for new art projects, paintings and inventions. Some of these ideas, such as his initial concept for the helicopter, informed future inventions.

Da Vinci's journals and notebooks are a reminder of the importance of generating ideas every day. His ideas showed us how we can better understand the world around us.

Scholar Michael Gelb studied da Vinci's notebooks and his life. Gelb recommends anyone who wants to become creative like da Vinci should make a habit of recording new ideas every day.

In *How to Think Like Leonardo da Vinci*, Gelb wrote:

> Busy lives and job responsibilities tend to drive us toward hard conclusions and measurable results, but the exploratory, free-flowing, unfinished, non-judgmental practice of keeping a da Vincian notebook encourages freedom of thought and expansion of perspective. In the manner of the maestro, don't worry about order and logical flow, just record.

You too should just record. Don't worry about being logical, tidy or organised, at least at first. Writing (and creativity) doesn't fit into tidy little boxes, so get into the habit of making a mess.

*Leonardo da Vinci's Vitruvian Man is one of his most
famous journal entries, via Luc Viatour / www.Lucnix.be
(2007)*

RAISE THE BAR

Get a pen and paper and write down 10 or even 100 ideas for whatever you're working on.

Don't judge, dismiss or censure whatever comes to mind. Instead, record your idea and progress quickly to the next one. The task of generating so many new ideas will force your brain to make new connections and mash up old ideas.

If you're struggling to come up with ideas, try writing down at least 10:

- Reasons why something will work/won't work
- Arguments why you're for/against something

- Ideas you can combine
- Things you need to do next
- Interviewees you could source
- Headlines
- Ways to open or close your story with a bang
- Questions you need answers to
- Unusual facts or pieces of information you possess
- Strengths/weaknesses of your chosen topic

Much like freewriting, don't worry about the quality of your ideas. Aim for quantity over quality. It's easier to generate 100 ideas of variable quality than it is to think of one perfect idea.

After you've captured 35 bad ideas, you stand a better chance of coming up with one great idea. Conversely, if you try to come up with one great idea for your writing project, you will struggle.

Raise the bar impossibly high and you will surprise yourself with what you can achieve.

At the very least, if you have more ideas to write about, you will find it easier to sit down in front of the blank page.

Every day, I write down 10 ideas for blog posts, articles, short stories or book chapters in my notebook.

Some of my ideas are terrible, and others never make it beyond my notebook. However, by the end of the week I have lots of new ideas I can sift through, and at least one always holds some value.

I might sound borderline obsessive about generating new ideas each day, but I don't want to run out of fuel when the time comes to write.

REVIEW YOUR IDEAS

After you get into the habit of generating new ideas, you'll have more than you can write about. The day lacks enough hours, and life carries too many commitments for you to write about everything you want.

Here's the thing:

Acting on an idea carries an opportunity cost. When you write about one idea, you're spending time that could be spent writing about something else.

For example, if I've got an idea for a blog post and an idea for a book chapter, I can only focus on one at a time. So, do I write the book chapter or the blog post?

The answer depends on my priorities and how good the idea is. If you want to decide what ideas are best to spend time on, ask yourself:

- Is this something I'm passionate about writing?
- Can I say something in a unique way about this topic?
- Is this idea newsworthy or popular online?
- Am I prepared to give up working on another idea to work on *this idea?*
- Do I have enough knowledge and research to hand to write about this idea in detail?

BE HONEST WITH YOURSELF

Several years ago, I spent a lot of time reviewing products, games, services and music for Irish newspapers. These articles were easy to write, I got to keep what I reviewed, and I enjoyed the process, at first.

Later though, I recognised I was criticising ideas other

people had created and worked on, and it's almost always easier to criticise than it is to create.

So, I told my editor I didn't want to review games, films or music albums anymore. I wanted to concentrate on writing news stories and feature articles. At least this kind of writing would give me room to come up with ideas and make better mistakes.

I'm not a journalist anymore, and I review products on my blog only if I'm passionate about the product or service and it can help writers accomplish more. I prefer spending my time writing longer, more involved articles that are challenging.

This pursuit is harder and more time-consuming, but it's also more satisfying.

Becoming a more productive writer means coming up with ideas every day and then spending time refining your ideas to an essential few. It means being honest about how you spend your precious creative time.

BUILD A PERSONAL LIBRARY OF GREAT IDEAS

"We judge it is of great service in studies. . . to bestow diligence and labor in setting down commonplaces; as it affords matter to invention, and collects and strengthens the judgment." – Francis Bacon

Productive writers keep a personal library where they store their best ideas, what they've learnt, information about what they've read and even notes on what they'd like to write next.

I'm not referring to building a spare room in your house that you fill with shelves and books.

Instead, you can create your personal library by keeping a commonplace book and a swipe file. You can also build one by annotating your favourite books and articles and writing down your ideas.

HOW TO KEEP A COMMONPLACE BOOK

A commonplace book will help you marshal research for

your writing projects. Before the digital age, commonplace books were popular.

They were a kind of personal, pre-internet repository of letters, medical information, quotes, facts, experiences, anecdotes and personal histories. They were also a way for individuals, families and communities to sort and store knowledge about their lives.

Historical figures, authors and poets such as Marcus Aurelius, Napoleon, Thomas Jefferson, Francis Bacon, John Milton and W.H. Auden all kept or published commonplace books.

More recently, American author Ryan Holiday explained how he uses a commonplace book to write his books.

He said,

> The purpose of the [commonplace] book is to record and organise these gems for later use in your life, in your business, in your writing, speaking or whatever it is that you do.

A commonplace book will help you become a more productive writer because when the time comes to write your next book or article, you will already have a resource of relevant information to draw on. You will be the kind of writer who is always researching, learning and on the hunt for new ideas.

You won't need to spend hours researching because you will already know what you want to write about. Your research will form part of your creative life.

A commonplace book works only if you read widely and mark what's relevant as you go. Then you must extract useful information and put it in your commonplace book. You can use a paper-based or digital system to store this information in your commonplace book.

Whatever your preference, categorise entries in your commonplace book with terms that apply to your work and your life.

For example, I use the term "blog" for ideas and articles that are relevant to blog posts I want to write. I use the term "journal" to record ideas and information for entries in my journal.

When I was writing this book, I categorised various entries in my commonplace book by terms related to each strategy.

To get value from your commonplace book, make a habit of regularly reviewing and reorganising your entries. This way, the wisdom you're gathering will sink into each of your writing projects.

HOW TO KEEP A SWIPE FILE

A swipe file is a place where you store facts, figures, sentences and ideas relating to your work. It's a repository of information that if not relevant to your current writing project,will be of use at some point in the future.

Copywriters and advertisers use swipe files all the time to keep ideas, research and information they can use for future campaigns.

Dan S. Kennedy is a legendary business author, copywriter and salesperson. He writes about swipe files,

> I built up huge "idea files"—samples of ads, mailings, and sales letters...You do not need much creativity to write letters; you only need to be adept at recycling and reorganising ideas, themes, words, and phrases.

I don't know about you, but I'd rather become adept at this craft than be the kind of person who grinds it out, project after project. If you're interested in learning more about copywriting, I explain how to write words in chapter 13.

If you keep a swipe file, the next time you have to write copy for a website, blog post, email or social media campaign, you can take information directly from your swipe file instead of having to come up with fresh ideas.

Maintaining swipe files means you can spend less time staring out of windows and more time accomplishing your non-fiction projects.

Don't think of swipe files as cheating. Lawyers keep boilerplate legal text they can use for future contracts and agreements.

Professional software developers store snippets of code that can be used for future projects. Even journalists keep quotes from interviewees that they can use for future news stories.

As with a commonplace book, you can keep a paper or digital swipe file. A paper swipe file could consist of newspaper and magazine clippings, as well as your notes that you store in a drawer next to your desk, or you could keep a digital swipe file using a tool like Evernote.

Here are some of the more popular kinds of information productive writers keep in their swipe files:

- Headlines
- Quotes
- Interviews with people in your area of interest
- Inspiring videos and pictures
- Random facts and figures
- Sketches
- Phone numbers
- Angles for blog posts
- Emails

- Writing prompts
- Great first lines
- Advertisements
- Social media posts
- Presentations

To get the most use from your swipe file, take time at the end of the week or before you're about to start a new writing project and see if you can extract useful ideas and turn them into something fresh.

ANNOTATE WHAT YOU READ

If you've ever picked up a dog-eared book from six or 12 months ago, you've probably had the experience of looking for half-remembered passages, quotations and arguments.

Annotating your favourite works means you can spend less time researching your current writing project and more time writing. This practice will help you critically engaging with whatever you're reading and ensure this information seeps deeper into your subconscious.

I annotate books by highlighting passages on my Kindle. I also record observations about what I've read in digital apps like Evernote.

There's nothing wrong with making notes using pen and paper. You can do this in a journal, or you can underline favourite sentences in books.

These highlights, bookmarks and annotations can become food for future works. They enable you to connect the concepts in one book to another and examine how the author's writings relate to your life or your work.

Some experts recommend writing a brief summary after finishing a chapter so you can assess the value of a book later. I use this method when I want to remember something–for an exam, for example–but I rarely do this when I'm reading for relaxation.

When I'm writing an article or blog post, I return to my annotations for inspiration, advice and sometimes to back up a point.

Prior to making annotations, I spent a lot of time searching old books for quotes that I half-remembered and points I wasn't sure about. Now I can save time on research and spend more time writing.

Getting into the habit of annotating what you read and love is a great way of emulating and learning from the writing techniques of more accomplished writers.

At the very least, annotations will help you consider what makes for a good sentence or argument and what makes for a poor one.

WRITE DOWN YOUR IDEAS

Many accomplished writers are fastidious about recording their ideas throughout the day.

Mark Twain carried a pocket notebook with him at all times to record his ideas.

Thomas Jefferson jotted down notes about everything from the growth of plants and flowers to observations about daily life.

Even George Lucas keeps a notebook with him when he's shooting a film.

The children's author Roald Dahl valued writing ideas down too. He said about his work, "A writer of fiction lives in fear. Each new day demands new ideas and he can never be sure whether he is going to come up with them or not."

Dahl famously wrote down the word "chocolate" into the dirt on his car, while stuck in traffic. He later turned this idea into the book *Charlie and the Chocolate Factory*.

Whether you use a commonplace book, a swipe file or just a notebook, get into the habit of writing your ideas down every day.

You can keep a portable notebook for recording ideas on the go. You can use digital tools like an app on your smartphone, or you can buy a small notebook that fits in your pocket.

Whatever your tool, your notebook should become an extension of yourself.

HOLD YOURSELF TO ACCOUNT

"When the beginnings of self-destruction enter the heart it seems no bigger than a grain of sand." – John Cheever

Holding yourself to account means taking time to see how your writing is progressing and if you are working on the right things. To follow this strategy, you must be realistic about your progress and growth as a writer and find a way to keep yourself honest.

Productive writers can use two great methods to hold themselves to account.

The first is to **set clear goals** for your writing projects that you track and make progress towards each week. This method is suited to people who like lists and clearly defined boundaries.

The second method is to **keep a journal** where you write introspective entries about your writing. This method is best suited for writers who dislike the confines of a To Do list but still require a way to review how their work is progressing.

In this chapter, I'll explain how you can use either method to hold yourself accountable.

SET GOALS FOR YOUR WRITING

Setting goals will give you something to work towards and help you eliminate nonessential tasks from your life. I like goals because they give a clear marker that I can make progress towards. In other words, I can either achieve a goal or miss it.

You can set goals for your writing easily. All you have to do is make sure they are SMART. That is:

(S)pecific: Be clear about what exactly you want to achieve. "I want to write a book" is not specific. "I want to publish a collection of children's short stories" is.

(M)easurable: Have a system for measuring your progress towards your goal each week or month.

(A)chievable: Pick a goal that you can accomplish. If you haven't written much before, you're unlikely to write a novel in three months no matter how productive you are.

(R)ealistic: You must have a reasonable chance of accomplishing your goal. Winning the Nobel Prize for Literature is an unrealistic goal for most of us.

(T)imed: Set a deadline for yourself that you can meet.

Here is one of my creative SMART goals:

I will self-publish (realistic) and sell (achievable) a short story collection (specific) by my birthday (timed, measurable).

Here's another SMART goal:

I will write 1,000 words a day or write 10 hours a week (measurable and specific) every week (achievable, realistic) before June 31 (timed).

KEEP TO DO LISTS

Now comes the nuts and bolts of doing your work.

Each of your creative projects should have an **outcome**, that is a statement of how you want things to turn out.

Next, write down all the actions that you need to take on a list to achieve this outcome.

You can keep a separate list for each project or you can keep one master list with your tasks organised by context.

When writing your "To Dos", use clear and specific active verbs so you don't have to think when you read them later on. Set deadlines for each of these actions in your calendar so you track what's coming up.

For example, when I'm planning my writing for the week, one of my action items will say, "Write a 1,000-word scene set in a restaurant on Thursday."

When I finish my blog post about productivity, my action item will say, "Email my latest blog post about productivity to my list by Wednesday."

Remember, you don't need to do everything on these lists. Instead, simply get everything down in one place so you don't waste mental energy thinking about what you need to do during the week.

Then, once a day, once a week or as often as is necessary, pick the most important tasks from these lists and do them.

At the end of each day, I pick the three most important things I need to do the following day and focus on accomplishing those tasks first thing.

So stick with the task at hand without overthinking what you're doing.

USE JOURNAL WRITING

Don't like goals or To Do lists?

Don't worry, lots of writers find them confining. You can use a simple writing practice to gain an insight into how your writing is progressing.

Keeping a journal will foster your creativity and help you write more often. It's also a great way of holding yourself to account.

Why?

Writing a journal can help you turn thoughts and feelings into words and ideas. Because a journal is private, you're less likely to censure yourself.

This kind of honest writing is key to improving your craft and expanding the boundaries of your writing. If you keep a journal for several years, older entries serve as signposts for how your writing is progressing.

You can keep a journal in a paper notebook, in a password-protected file on your computer or by using one of the many journal apps available for smartphones.

In it, you could describe how your current writing project is progressing, what's holding you back and your plans for future. You could also use your journal to note sentences that you'd like to use and to tease out ideas for your writing projects.

American novelist and short story writer John Cheever kept one of the best journals of the 20th century, and he wrote like one good friend talking to another. Throughout his life, he chronicled his difficult marriage, his loneliness, sexuality, alcoholism and decline.

Virginia Woolf was also fastidious about her journal writing as a means of holding herself to account. In an entry dated 1919, she described how journal writing encouraged and improved her craft.

I believe that during the past year I can trace some increase of ease in my professional writing which I attribute to my casual hours after tea.

My life isn't much like Cheever's or Woolf's, but I learnt a lot about the art of journal writing from both authors.

Keeping a journal doesn't mean recording a daily summary of one's life. Anyone interested in writing a journal should expose themselves entirely in their journal and seek out brutal honestly.

I write about what I accomplished and failed at recently and what I'm thinking about. I also write about ideas for future writing projects. Some of my journal entries are only one or two lines long.

My shortest entry simply reads "Exhausted" (did I mention that I have two small children?).

Others run several paragraphs or even pages in length.

The journals of Cheever and writers like Vladimir Nabokov taught me that keeping a journal helps identify negative patterns, thoughts and behaviours. In a way, journal writing is like the all-seeing eye of Sauron in *Lord of the Rings*. You can't hide, and you can't run from it.

Woolf writes about her depression at length in her journals. In 1934, she describes the period after she finished her experimental novel *The Waves*. "I was, I remember, nearer suicide, seriously, than since 1913."

Cheever chronicles his alcoholism at length in his journal, and I felt a sense of relief when he writes about finally becoming sober.

I don't want to be too morbid here.

The journals of these authors aren't all filled with dark life lessons and lamentations.

Nabokov, the author of *Lolita*, writes at length about his love for his mother and father, his son and Russia of old. And

I've yet to read a more powerful personal mission statement than Cheever's aspiration for the blank page.

> To write well, to write passionately, to be less inhibited, to be warmer, to be more self-critical, to recognise the power of as well as the force of lust, to write, to love.

KEEP A SENSE DIARY

Keeping a sense diary or journal is a useful practice for more creative writers who want to hold onto their experiences and ideas. In this diary, record experience that triggered your senses of touch, taste sound, or smell per day.

You could write about how a meal tasted or what a person's voice sounded like. You may also notice the stickiness of sweet tea, the coarseness of an unvarnished floor and the pain behind your eyes when you're tired. The world is your source material.

Then see if you can remix your sense diary to describe how a smell tasted or what a sound looks like. This may sound daft, but it's an unusually effective creative trick.

Synaesthesia is an accepted process for perceiving one sense in terms of another. It is also common practice for creative writers to remix and play on readers' perceptions of the five senses in their works.

Nabokov described to the BBC in 1962 how he could hear colours in different languages.

He said, "The long 'a' of the English alphabet has for me the tint of weathered wood, but a French 'a' evokes polished ebony."

GOING WITH WHAT WORKS

I set goals for each of my writing projects, and I keep a journal. I set goals because this keeps me honest and I find some comfort and security in having a To Do list that I can review, tick off and manage.

I also keep a journal. I like journal writing because it allows me to practice writing when I want to do anything but, and when I reread older entries I can unearth problems in my creative and even my personal life.

Use what works for you and abandon what doesn't.

STUCK? KEEP READING

"Either write something worth reading or do something worth writing." – Benjamin Franklin

German blacksmith Johannes Gutenberg invented the printing press sometime before 1450. His invention enabled the printing of lengthy texts that people used to spread their ideas.

In 1518, theologian Martin Luther used Gutenberg's invention to print German copies of his Latin book *95 Theses*.

The subsequent popularity of this book across Europe became a driving force of the Protestant Reformation.

Gutenburg's printing press enabled the dissemination of ideas that opened people's minds to new ways of thinking and looking at the world, and it's a classic example of just how powerful ideas and books are.

If you want to become a better and more productive writer, read frequently and outside of your comfort zone.

Reading and writing have a symbiotic relationship. Through reading, you will discover stories, facts and arguments for your work, and you will find new ideas and make connections that improve your writing.

Bulgarian writer and critic Maria Popova described this process as "combinatorial creativity." She wrote:

> ...in order for us to truly create and contribute to the world, we have to be able to connect countless dots, to cross-pollinate ideas from a wealth of disciplines, to combine and recombine these pieces and build new castles.

Even if you read for pleasure, every time you open a book, you make an unconscious deposit in your memory bank of ideas.

However, if you don't read at all, the next time you turn up in front of the blank page your memory bank of ideas will be empty, and writing anything meaningful will feel almost impossible.

HOW BENJAMIN FRANKLIN WORKED

Benjamin Franklin is famous productive genius.

As one of the United States founding fathers, he used the printing press to spread his ideas, and he even invented a more modern version of this device to grow his printing business.

Alongside work, Franklin put aside several hours every morning and evening for reading and self-examination.

Each morning he asked himself: "What good shall I do today?" Franklin also advocated a daily 'air bath' instead of bathing in cold water.

He said about air baths,

> I rise early almost every morning, and sit in my chamber

without any clothes whatever, half an hour or an hour, according to the season, either reading or writing.

This practice is not in the least painful, but on the contrary, agreeable; and if I return to bed afterwards, before I dress myself, as sometimes happens, I make a supplement to my night's rest, of one or two hours of the most pleasing sleep that can be imagined.

Air baths won't help you write (or keep clean for that matter), but Franklin's life demonstrates how we can manage our downtime and incorporate important activities like reading and self-examination into our busy days.

For example, many people read at the end of the day. That's fine, but if you have a job and family commitments, you may lack the energy or patience for a challenging read.

This, perhaps, is one reason why Benjamin Franklin made time for reading in the morning and afternoon. Remember, as a productive writer it's smart to be mindful of your energy levels.

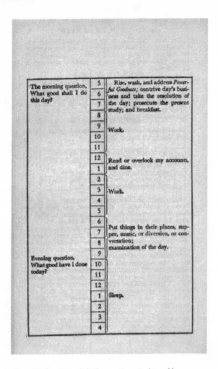

The morning question, What good shall I do this day?	5	Rise, wash, and address *Powerful Goodness*; contrive day's business and take the resolution of the day; prosecute the present study; and breakfast.
	6	
	7	
	8	
	9	Work.
	10	
	11	
	12	Read or overlook my accounts, and dine.
	1	
	2	
	3	Work.
	4	
	5	
	6	Put things in their places, supper, music, or diversion, or conversation; examination of the day.
	7	
	8	
	9	
Evening question, What good have I done today?	10	
	11	
	12	
	1	Sleep.
	2	
	3	
	4	

Benjamin Franklin's original daily routine via http://www.usgennet.org/

FIND TIME TO READ

Some people say they'd like to read more, but they don't have the time or energy.

If you're having this problem, carve out small parts of the day when you have the energy or time to read, such as first thing in the morning.

You can also take advantage of those random blocks of free time that life sometimes presents, such as the unexpected 20-minute wait in the doctor's office, railway station or airport.

If you get into the habit of carrying a book or e-reader, you can read during a lunch break, over breakfast, after dinner or while waiting for an appointment.

Committing to read at least 20 pages every day is another great way of setting yourself up for success. After all, if you can't find time to read 20 pages, then how can you find time to write? Similarly, if you drive to work, you can read more by listening to audiobooks during your commute.

I love reading, but like many people I browse the internet when I should be reading, or I end up reading the wrong book altogether.

Let me explain.

When I read about a book that sounds interesting, this thought leads to an "I'd love to read that book, but I have to read this book first" moment.

Then I invariably forget the name of the interesting book. Keeping a running list of books I want to read helped me overcome this problem.

If you do this, when you're stuck for something to read, you can consult your list before you buy. Such a method shortcuts wandering around a virtual or bricks and mortar bookshop and buying a book because the cover, reviews or discounts are impressive.

STOP AFTER THE FIRST 50 PAGES

Oprah Winfrey advises if you're 50 pages into a book and not enjoying it, put the book down.

The world contains so many good books – and more than anyone can read in one lifetime – so why waste time reading a book because you feel like you should?

You can take Winfrey's advice farther by reading samples that Amazon and other stores offer for free before you buy a book.

Some heavy readers advise concentrating on one book at

a time because this increases your chances of finishing one book and moving on to the next.

I disagree.

Reading several books at once means you can alternate books when one becomes tiresome or a slog.

Then, you can return to the first book when you feel refreshed. For this method to work, read books from several different genres or combine fiction and non-fiction.

Personally, I find non-fiction books are best suited for daytime reading while fiction books make for ideal night-time reading. I've also found reading three books at once feels about right; any more becomes overwhelming.

WAIT FOR A GREAT SENTENCE

Sometimes, I read several books at once over the course of a week or two. On other occasions, I go several weeks without reading any long-form works. This drought isn't because I don't want to read; it's because the challenges of a day-to-day life get in the way.

I used to feel guilty about these breaks from consuming the written word, but now I accept them because I know I will return to a bookstore with my list and a belief that a great sentence is waiting.

Reading, like any activity, has its peaks and troughs, and rather than beating yourself up about not reading, accept you won't always have free time to read. And if you hate the damn book, put it down and start something new, something better.

As a productive writer, you must read books that fall inside and outside your comfort zone.

You can do this by carving out reading time in your day, making the most of those random blocks of free time we all have and by keeping track of what you want to read.

GET PERMISSION LATER

"Never ask permission, ask for forgiveness later." – James Altucher

Many people say they to want write, but then they make excuses. They say things like:

"I'm not good enough to write a book. Nobody will ever want to read it."

Or

"I've got nothing to write about. I need to find more ideas and do more research."

Or

"Writing is just too hard. I was always bad at English in school and I've no idea how to become a good writer."

Instead of waiting for some anointed writing guru to give you permission to write, start today.

You already have what you need.

START NOW

School teaches almost nothing about writing beyond how to read and spell. You can learn many things about writing by reading voraciously.

You don't need years of life experience either; American disability activist and author Helen Keller published *The Story of My Life* when she was 22.

If you pick up the pen and sit down in front of the blank page, you are good enough simply because you've moved past the point of procrastination. This act is no small feat.

Today, successful writers don't need as much talent or luck as writers like Updike or Hemingway had.

We can write a blog post, article or book and then self-publish it. If we write, we can take advantage of the digital tools that our predecessors didn't have and share our work almost instantly with an audience.

You can write for someone's website, start your blog or self-publish a book on Amazon.

Don't wait for someone to give you permission.

Writing consumes a lot of time, but you can recover this back eliminating passive activities in your day. Television, casual internet browsing, social media and staying up late into the night—I'm looking at you.

After you eliminate time-wasters and get into the habit of regularly writing, your mind will fill the vacuum with new and more fantastic ideas clamouring for space on the page in front of you.

If something you have to do is more important than writing, ask yourself why you want to write in the first place and then decide what's more important. It's going to be hard work, but most worthwhile things are.

As soon as you turn up in front of the blank page with a desire to say something, anything, you're already ahead.

Stop making excuses and pick up the pen. Later, if you find the whole process a waste of time, you can cross writing off your list and move on with your life.

LEARN TO WRITE FOR YOURSELF

Writing isn't a shortcut to celebrity or riches.

If that's your goal, you will find rewards far quicker by concentrating on other professions. I'm not suggesting writers should starve, but you must be passionate about your work.

A love of the craft will sustain you when others criticise and reject your work.

This passion will drive you when you're struggling to make money from your words. And if you are passionate enough, you will keep seeking ways to improve even when you're exhausted, frustrated and broken.

If, on the other hand, you're not passionate about your writing, why should your readers care?

Write for yourself first, write something you enjoy reading and write something that makes you regard a page of wet ink (or a screen of pixels), a page you filled, with pride.

Use the life of J.D. Salinger as an example.

After the success of *The Catcher in the Rye*, Salinger withdrew from public view. In 1953, two years after the publication of his famous book, Salinger left New York and moved to a remote, 90-acre place in Cornish, New Hampshire.

He continued to write, but this time for himself, and some of these stories were published only after his death in 2010.

Others remain unpublished.

Salinger loved what he did, and he didn't care if people read his works.

DON'T WAIT

I once coached a non-fiction writer about how he could focus on his work and write 1,000 words a day.

We talked about how he could use a productivity strategy to eliminate distractions and increase his daily word count. I asked this writer to eliminate distractions for where he works and hold himself to account. (See chapter six).

I think the writer was happy with how our coaching call went because afterwards he emailed me to say thanks.

At the bottom of his email he wrote, "The other helpful thing was the sense of legitimacy as a writer I got from talking with you."

I was happy to get positive feedback like this – I'm human after all! – and to know I was able to help him.

But something didn't sit right with me. The more I thought about our conversation, the more I realised I'd missed an important point. This writer was already doing his most important work before he had ever talked to me. He is well on his way. If you wrote today, you are too.

Whatever kind of writer you are, you don't need affirmation from me or anyone else to call yourself a writer or to feel like what you are doing is worthwhile.

If you have the guts to turn up every day, sit down in the chair and do the hard work of putting one word after another onto the blank page even when you know what you're saying might not be any good, then you are a writer.

Don't ask for permission.

Don't wait for someone to tell you what you're doing is worthwhile.

And don't do it just for the money.

I spent most of my early twenties looking for affirmation from accomplished writers and professional editors. I paid for writing courses and I made a point of getting closer to editors who I knew were better than I. Sometimes I got the affirmation I was after, but more often than not I didn't.

Either way, I still had to sit down in front of the blank page alone, get the words down and figure out a way to get better.

Every day, I try to do what writers like Natalie Goldberg recommend. "Write what disturbs you, what you fear, what you have not been willing to speak about. Be willing to be split open."

I still feel like giving up some days. I almost gave up last week.

I'm still trying to figure out this strange job of ours.

Writing is often a lonely craft, and it sometimes helps to talk to other writers about a problem you're having on the blank page.

We all need support and critical feedback to overcome our problems from time to time. Being recognised by other writers feels great when your motivation is waning. Similarly, hiring an editor is a surefire way to improve your craft.

I love getting comments and emails from readers who have opinions and even nice things to say about my work.

I keep them in a file in my computer and reread them when I feel like quitting.

I'd like to tell you I don't feel like quitting very often, but I'd be lying.

These comments and emails keep me going when I want to stop. And I must keep putting one word after another because this is what we do.

To become a productive writer, turn up for, write and go after what you want day after day.

Even if you win the lotto tomorrow, and your money worries disappear, even if you're the lone survivor of a nuclear holocaust, sit down and do your most important work.

Do it because there's an ache inside you that only writing can soothe.

Do it because you can't imagine doing anything else.

Do it because to write is to create and to create is to live.

Anything else isn't an option.

STEAL FROM THE GREATS

"Good artists copy, great artists steal." – Pablo Picasso

Are you a thief?

If you're a writer or in any way creative, you should be.

More than seven billion people are alive on this planet today, to say nothing of those who went before us. To think your idea is original is to ignore the weight of history. *The Bible* has been done, *War and Peace* is over, and Moby Dick has been harpooned.

I'm not special. My ideas are far from original. I wrote *The Savvy Writer's Guide to Productivity* because I've read so much good, bad and unusual advice about productivity and writing over the years.

I wanted to put it down on the blank page and remix it with my voice and experiences. I wanted to learn from my idols and create something that would help readers, that would help you.

So I stole.

I'm not the first person to confess this crime.

Take Apple's co-founder, Steve Jobs. He is widely acknowledged as one of the most creative innovators of the past 50 years, but Jobs stole like crazy, and he openly admitted it.

You can see Jobs in a viral YouTube video explaining why creative people steal.

He said, "Picasso had a saying—'good artists copy, great artists steal'—and we have always been shameless about stealing great ideas."

Jobs is widely credited as the inventor of the portable music player or iPod, but he wasn't the first person to invent a portable music player; the boffins at Sony were.

Jobs wasn't the first person to invent a tablet either; BlackBerry and IBM designed dozens of models before the iPad.

Instead, Jobs took ideas already in existence and remixed them with his voice. He took old ideas and transformed them into better ones.

Don't waste time sitting around stroking your chin, gazing at the night sky and trying to come up with something original.

Somebody, somewhere has already written or thought about what you're about to say. Your challenge as a productive writer is to take an old idea, add your voice and transform it.

HOW TO EMULATE YOUR HEROES

The productive writer learns faster by emulating his heroes.

This process is different from stealing or copying from them. When you emulate, you make a conscious decision to take apart the work of writers you admire and reassemble it using your voice and ideas.

This educational process will help you discover how accomplished writers succeed and fail on the blank page, and it will help you finish what you're working on.

"At some point, you'll have to move from imitating your heroes to emulating them," Austin Kleon wrote in *Steal Like an Artist*.

When a mechanic wants to figure out an engine, he or she sometimes spends hours taking it apart and putting it back together. This process helps the mechanic see how the engine works and even what's wrong with it.

If you want to learn from your favourite writer, pick a work you admire. Take it apart sentence by sentence and ask yourself:

- How does the writer make you feel throughout the piece?
- Where does the writer use the first, second or third person?
- Does the writer address you directly or indirectly? How does this make you feel?
- How much of the work is fact, fiction or embellishment?
- How does the writer manage to convey their opinions or arguments?
- How does the writer begin and end each sentence, paragraph or chapter?
- Do you agree with what the author is saying or could you say it differently? If so, how?
- How does the writer introduce a topic and arrive at a conclusion?
- When does the writer repeat and idea and why?
- What kind of journey does the writer bring you on?

- Why has the writer structured his or her work one way and not the other?

You can do this by writing out the stories of your idols line by line, by annotating their work or even by extracting key quotes and ideas and putting them into your swipe file or commonplace book for future use.

Disassembling and reassembling the work of your heroes will help you figure out how they construct their sentences, paragraphs, chapters and ideas.

This creative process is time-consuming, but it will help you develop your voice for writing and give you an insight into how other writers work.

WHAT I STOLE

American poet, novelist and short story writer Charles Bukowski is one of my creative idols.

His brash style of poetry makes me feel like he's picking a fight with me, and I've always been fascinated by his honest portrayals of writing, creativity, the drudgery of work and his relationships with women.

I took his work apart line by line by writing down key lines from his poems and using them as fragments and ideas for entries in my journal. I even used one of his poems as inspiration for a short story.

Short story writer Raymond Carver is another creative idol of mine. I've spent hours reading and rereading his collection of short stories, *What We Talk About When We Talk About Love* and *Cathedral.*

I tried to mimic his manner of writing sparse and clean sentences and studied how he portrays a character, a scene and a major plot point. I used what Carver knew about the art of the short story to expose weaknesses in my work.

My efforts at reconstruction fell short on both counts, but I discovered I'm more comfortable writing in the first person and using everyday language. I found out more about the mechanics of a great story, and I discovered the nuggets of ideas for my fiction and non-fiction.

STEAL RESPONSIBLY

The next time a writer impresses you, read them closely, emulate what they do and steal their best ideas.

I'm not advocating a cut-and-paste job; instead take what they've done and remix it with your voice. If you take only from one writer, it's outright theft, but if you take from the many, it's creative.

Use the creative hard work of your idols to provide a foundation for what you're going to write. Prop your ideas on the foundations of their hard work. Cite your sources and wear your inspirations on your sleeve if you need to.

Don't be ashamed about what you're doing. Creativity exists somewhere between a stolen idea and your inner voice.

You can use that.

DECIDE WHAT'S ESSENTIAL

"You cannot overestimate the unimportance of practically everything." – Greg McKeown

How often do you get the right things done?

By the right things I mean writing your book, articles and stories. Once you've taken care of your family and the bills, it's up to you to write.

It's up to you to decide what's essential.

According to Greg McKeown, author of *Essentialism: The Disciplined Pursuit of Less*, an essentialist removes the trivial and focuses on what adds value.

Essentialists make smart decisions about how to spend their time, energy and resources because they understand this is the best way of contributing more to the people in their lives, their families and society. That sounds a lot like what the productive writer does too.

I've discovered five important questions that are helping me make progress towards getting more of the right things done. And I want to share them with you.

Q. Is this Activity Adding Value to My Life?

Since I was a child, I played and loved video games. When I was in my mid-twenties, I even reviewed them for a popular entertainment website.

The website didn't pay me, but I didn't care. I enjoyed gaming, and I was able to keep the games after I wrote my reviews.

After a year or two, I felt a shift in how I approached games. Instead of looking forward to playing the next AAA title or blockbuster release, I began to dread the tedious missions, the walkthroughs, and inevitable write-ups.

So I sold my games, gave my console to my son and abandoned my hobby.

I'm not making a case against gaming; instead, I share this example of how we value our time differently as writers mature.

Perhaps you have old hobbies which you no longer enjoy. Or maybe you could cut back on the hours you spend at the office seeking promotion. If it's not adding value to your life, consider if you can remove it and use this extra time to write.

Q. How am I Going to Fill My Glass?

Consider your entire day as a glass.

As Stephen Covey notes, you can fill this glass with important activities or big rocks, such as spending time with family or working on projects you're passionate about.

Then, you can fill the glass with nonessential activities like answering email or watching television. These are like grains of sand, and they will settle around the big rocks in your day.

If you fill your glass with non-essential activities first, there will be no room left for the big rocks in your day.

Every night before I go to bed, I ask myself what I want to fill my glass with.

My answer is almost always the same: to write.

Unless I act, grains of sand will fill my day and leave no room for writing. However, if I make a conscious decision to write, grains of sand settle around the big rocks in my day.

I'm not going to lie and say I fit writing into every day, but when I do I feel lighter. And if I write first thing – even if it's just a journal entry – I don't have the inevitable moment when I sit on the couch after an exhausting and demanding day and think, "Oh no, I still have to write."

If you're not a writer, you still have big rocks in your life.

Examples include spending time with a loved one, meditating, exercising and work. Your grains of sand might be commitments you've made to others who aren't adding value to your life or passive activities like watching the news or reading social media feeds.

Decide on your big rocks before you go to bed, and you will wake up and fill your day with what matters.

Q. What Clutter Can I Eliminate?

Two years ago, I lost a dream job. I was unemployed for six months and spent my free time figuring out what matters most to me and reading about essentialism.

Essentialism felt like something I could get into, and when you're unemployed, you need something to get into. I learnt the quickest way to get started is to eliminate material goods you don't use, need, love or depend on.

I sold my laptop because I prefer to write using my desktop computer. I donated every book to charity that I promised myself I'd read but had no intention of doing.

I got rid of every item of clothing that I hadn't worn during the past 12 months. And I deleted almost all of the unwatched films and TV shows on my hard drive and cancelled my online subscriptions.

After I found a job, I thought of buying a new laptop and

replacing the clothes I'd given away. But I found I didn't miss any of those things.

Eliminating clutter gave me more space, more time and more room for the big rocks in my life.

Q. How Do I Protect Myself?

To be an essentialist is to protect your physical, mental and spiritual health. Each of these areas represents one side of a triangle, and if one is under stress, the other two will suffer.

To look after my mental health, I expose myself to new ideas by reading challenging books and recording 10 ideas every day based on those books. This practice, as recommended by the writer James Altucher, keeps my brain active.

For managing my my physical health, I run up to 20 miles each week. This practice helps me work through stressful problems, and it gives me more energy for other areas of my life.

To protect my spiritual health, I meditate for an hour or two each week, and I write regular journal entries about what I'm struggling with and grateful for.

I find these practices exceptionally difficult, but taking a step back from the trenches of the working week helps me quiet my monkey mind. It helps me sleep better at night. And then I can return to whatever I'm doing with a renewed vigour.

Q: How Often Do I Disconnect?

Several years ago, I went on vacation to a campsite in Italy. The campsite lacked reliable internet access, and I wasn't able to check my phone and my feeds or read the news whenever I wanted.

On the first day of this trip, I felt disconnected and behind. My hands kept reaching for the email app on my phone even though I knew I didn't have access to the internet.

After a day or two this habit died, and I began to enjoy those disconnected few days away from home. I took one lesson home from that holiday.

Being constantly connected kills my opportunity to escape, enjoy a vacation, spend time with the people I'm with and even focus on my work.

It's been awhile since I've gone a week without email, but I've removed the email app from my phone and check it only at predefined periods during the day.

I've also disabled as many notifications as possible on the devices I use. And I regularly work without being connected to the internet.

If you take regular time out to take care of yourself, you will be better able to focus on what matters.

LIVE YOUR WILD AND PRECIOUS LIFE

Essentialists avoid spending time on tasks they can say avoid, people they should say no to, and compromises that aren't worth making.

They are committed to working on what inspires them, what they're talented at, and pursuing their contributions to the world.

I'm still working on becoming an essentialist and eliminating the trivial from my life. I find the practices of essentialism difficult, but I know the productive writer can live their wild and precious life if they're brave enough.

LEARN TO SAY NO

"It takes determination, it takes a willingness to say 'no' and it can take time. But it will pay off in so many ways, for the rest of your life." – Leo Babauta

What's the biggest barrier between you and a finished piece of work?

Look in the mirror.

The day never seems to have enough hours. If you're like most people, you probably have too many personal and professional commitments to balance writing with other ambitions.

The vast majority of us have far more going on in our lives than we realise. All these commitments and projects carry a psychic weight.

This mental fatigue slows your progress and complicates reaching the end of whatever you're working on.

For example, can you concentrate at length on your novel or book if you also have to manage a large DIY project?

If you attend a late dinner with friends and go for drinks

afterwards, will you be able to rise early in the morning to write?

How productive will you be on the blank page if you've already worked overtime to pay for a new television?

Learning to say no to internal and external commitments is key to becoming a more productive writer.

If you decide to learn a new language, develop a new skill or take up a new hobby, you are taking time away from writing.

These new hobbies and skills might add value to your life, and you might be able to juggle your commitments, but writing is a demanding mistress who needs your attention. Can you afford to spend your valuable free time elsewhere?

Every new project you begin represents time you won't spend in front of the blank page. These new commitments can clog your creative bandwidth and reduce your ability to focus on the blank page.

By saying no, you can protect the parts of your day that you spend writing and concentrate on finishing what you started.

In *Daily Rituals: How Artists Work*, Mason Currey describes how French novelist Marcel Proust "made a conscious decision in 1910 to withdraw from society" and concentrate on his work.

Curry notes Pablo Picasso and his girlfriend, Fernande Olivier, regarded Sunday as an "at home" day, free from the obligations of friendship.

You don't need to be a recluse to become a more productive writer. Instead, consider how you're spending your time and if the result is worth the effort.

APPLY PARETO'S PRINCIPLE

In 1906, Italian economist Vilfredo Pareto found that 80 percent of the land in Italy was owned by 20 percent of the people.

Today, Pareto's Principle is the approach that anyone, including writers, can use to become more productive. It states that 20 percent of what we do provides 80 percent of the value we experience in our lives.

As described in chapter 10, consider what activities in your life are meaningful and what you can eliminate or reduce.

Your goal should be to concentrate on those 20 percent activities that give you 80 percent of the value you experience.

For example, it's more productive to spend an hour every day writing than spending this hour promoting your work on social media.

Look for secondary activities you can eliminate from your life too.

Examples include: watching television, browsing social media sites, comfort eating, online shopping and so on.

Indie authors Johnny B. Truant and Sean Platt address this point in their self-publishing guide *Write. Publish. Repeat: The No Luck Required Guide to Self-Publishing Success.*

> Eighty-percent activities are writing more and better books, building a moderate amount of reader engagement (efficiently, not via long emails), creating solid calls to action that lead people to your next books from the backs of those they've just finished, completing bundles and product funnels...and so on.

When I'm writing, I reduce the amount of time spent

watching television, gaming and browsing my favourite websites so I can spend more time writing.

I don't always succeed, but Pareto's Principle helps me refocus.

For example, when I began building an online platform for my writing, I became preoccupied with learning to code. I spent hours teaching myself HTML, CSS, JavaScript and the backend of WordPress.

I also took online classes in Illustrator, Photoshop and other design applications. I wrote reviews about my experiences and even considered started a blog about coding.

What happened?

I learnt something of effective design, but I also had less time to write the kind of prose that inspires me, and I produced fewer blog posts and articles.

I was putting more time and effort into design and coding activities and experiencing less meaningful results. I've never had ambitions to become a serious coder or designer and these activities were side attractions.

Now, I outsource any technical aspects to my blog on sites like Upwork. I also spend less time concerning myself with the design of my site.

Instead, I rely on premium WordPress themes and plugins that take care of the hard work for me. This way I can spend more time writing and finish what I started.

Before you say yes to your next project, consider if the project is part of the 20 percent that will provide real value later on.

USE NO TO GET MORE DONE

If you want to become a more productive writer, make friends with the word no.

Using this word will help you avoid getting

distracted, get out of unnecessary commitments and spend more time writing. Saying no to nonessential tasks will enable you to become a more productive writer.

So what should you say no to?

The Wrong Writing Projects

For several years, I reviewed products and services I had no interest in because a newspaper paid me for the work. This mindless writing stopped me creating the kinds of fiction and non-fiction that inspires me.

As a writer, you'll have many chances to exercise your creative muscles.

It might feel good to write an email, a page of copy or even an article, as we all need to get paid. However, what are your larger ambitions for the blank page?

Is your current writing project going to help you achieve your goals?

So-So Ideas

The more often you write, the more connections your brain will make between pieces of information you pick up during the day.

Your brain will spit out topics to write about, projects to take on and opportunities to purse. Some ideas will be good and some terrible.

It's easy to refuse a terrible or a daft idea, but it's harder to refuse a good idea.

If you pursue every good idea, you won't have time or space for the great ideas.

The next time you've got a good idea, ask if it's worth pursuing and if it's something you should be writing about.

New Writing Tools

Confession: I love new writing tools.

I've spent hours testing writing apps, online services and even the perfect desk and chair.

Like many new writers, I find the tools of the craft exciting to discover.

Some tools help me become more productive, but when I start using a new tool for the first time, it interrupts the flow of writing.

These tools are side attractions that distract from the main event.

Boring Books

Are you reading a boring book? Are you past page 50? Put it down and move onto something more exciting.

Get out of the genres that make you feel at home and away from your old reliable authors.

They have their purpose, but creative people go in search of fresh and challenging ideas. They find them in unexpected places, by reading challenging genres for example.

Unproductive Habits

Do you stay up late at night watching television? Is Facebook taking up your time. Or perhaps you're spending your attention checking emails on your phone.

These unproductive habits are draining your mental energy.

Consider using social media only at predetermined periods and removing email entirely from your phone and making a commitment to your creative work over all else.

HOW TO SAY NO LIKE A PRO

Now you have an idea of what to say no to, but how can you do it without offending your spouse, boss or friend?

If you're a professional writer, part of your job is to tell your editor about your commitments.

Then if your editor asks you to work on something you can politely decline and point to your commitments.

Do less but better.

If what you're writing is more personal, communicate clearly to friends and family members that you write at a certain time every morning or every night.

Stephen King describes this in *On Writing: A Memoir of the Craft*, saying writers must "write with the door closed."

At first, family might come to you during these times to ask a question or make a request, but if you explain your passion and they see your commitment, the people close to you will respect the time you're spending writing.

GUARD YOUR TIME

As a productive writer, the word no is your most powerful weapon against the time-consuming demands of daily life.

You can use the word no to keep meaningless activities from filling your day and to prioritise what's important in your life. Saying no will help you become the productive writer you're meant to be.

WRITE WITHOUT FEAR OR FAVOUR

"I wrote and wrote without pause without consciousness of my surroundings hour after hour. I felt a different person...I didn't feel frustrated or shut up anymore. I was free, I could think, I could live, I could create..." – Christy Brown

Some people love you.

Other people hate you.

Most people don't care.

Readers have so much to pick from, and your voice is just one of many shouting, "Choose me."

The glut of information is why you should never hold back when you write.

If you tone down an article because you're afraid of what people will think, remember that most people are too wrapped up in their lives to care about one more blog post, article or book. Yes, some of your friends and family might take issue with what you've got to say, but you're not writing to impress them.

You could take the easy road and try to convince people that you're a good or honest person, but if this results in a bland, generic work, you've wasted your time.

If you convince a reader to spend time with you, respect that they're giving finite hours of their life to you.

Whatever you have to say, it better be damned good.

The next time you sit in front of the blank page or screen, forget your reader's reactions. Write without fear of what your reader will think of you. If you find this difficult, you could:

- Write about your fears and use this as an entry point into your work.
- Accept fear as a form of perfectionism that must be confronted.
- Acknowledge your fears, accept them and write what you want.
- Write a letter to a friend explaining what you're afraid about and then burn it.
- Remember what the goal of your writing project is. Then move towards this goal one action or sentence at a time.

If you come across as compassionate and caring, so be it. If you come across as angry and insensitive, so be it. As a writer, you must call out to readers and convince them to spend time with you.

If your writing is honest, it will be far more engaging than a piece where a writer holds back on revealing some essential truth because they're worried what others will think.

DON'T HIDE

If you use writing to hide yourself, then why should I spend time with you?

You know the kinds of writing I'm talking about.

You can find it on the promotional materials that came with your last bank statement or utility bill. You can read it on government documents and healthcare informational leaflets. It's there on thousands of corporate and institutional websites.

I've nothing against words that sell. (See chapter 13). I'm criticising joyless, staid writing that's full of passive verbs, awkward nouns and which doesn't speak to readers or customers.

It comes from a world where nobody does anything to anyone and no one cares. Bland writing tells me things firstly, and secondly, in hindsight, in conclusion, and after further deliberation.

These kinds of writing won't entertain, inform, inspire, educate or sell.

All of it belongs in the bin.

I want to hear the writer's problems and how they overcame them. I want to taste blood and feel the grit between my fingers. I want to take the author's outstretched hand and go on a journey. As a customer, I want you to speak to my problems.

I'm going to give you my time; don't waste it.

The best writers reveal some essential truth about the human condition; the rest of us aspiring authors can at least reveal some truth about ourselves.

I'm not asking you to slip into the confessional mode for every piece of writing; just don't make excuses for producing senseless copy that's devoid of life.

Even if you're writing copy for your business, don't bore

me with paragraphs about your product's technical features. Don't expect me to sit through a thousand words of passive verbs, adjectives and nouns nobody ever says.

How are you going to solve my problems? Can you save me money or help me spend more time with my family?

Show me how I can become rich or successful like you.

Tell me something true.

WITNESS WHAT CHRISTY BROWN DID

Christy Brown is one of Ireland's most famous writers and artists.

He grew up in inner-city Dublin during the middle of the twentieth century, and he had cerebral palsy.

Brown was depressed for much of his life because of his disability and subsequent alcoholism.

He grew up in a large family where he struggled to get attention because of his disability.

So with his mother's help, he learnt to write with his left foot. Later, as a young man, Brown wrote the famous memoir *My Left Foot*. He also published his groundbreaking novel *Down All the Days*.

In *My Left Foot* Brown abandoned himself entirely to portraying what it was like to grow up with cerebral palsy and how his real disability lay in the reactions of those around him.

In *Down All the Days,* Brown abandoned himself entirely to portraying how cruel, illogical and hard life was in Dublin during the mid-twentieth century.

Today, the significance of *My Left Foot* and *Down All the Days* might be understated, but their power and honesty remain intact. They are essential reading for anyone concerned with disability or Irish literature.

Brown offers more than just a glimpse of how he lived

with disability; he expands our view of the world, and he reveals a fundamental part of the human condition.

When Brown picked up his pen with his left foot, he abandoned himself entirely to the written word.

Both works contain a big idea, and even if you, the reader aren't prepared to climb on board, Brown commits himself entirely.

Although he never quite overcame his depression, he found a new, inner life through his creations and expressions on the blank page. Today Brown's readers can continue share in his life long after his death in 1981.

Any aspiring writer can think and live and create on the blank page. We can stop making excuses and abandon ourselves to an idea. We can all learn from Brown.

MY STRUGGLE WITH FEAR

When I was in my early twenties, I told people I wanted to write a book. There was just one problem. I wasn't writing anything, at all.

I believed I wasn't ready to write and that I needed some anointed mentor to pull me aside and say, "Bryan, now is your time."

I became jealous of the success of people around me and grew sick of my lack of progress. So I joined a fiction and non-fiction writing workshop in Dublin. On the second evening, the instructor said every student had to submit a short story.

I was afraid.

I hadn't written a short story in years, but I didn't want the class or the instructor to know.

A writer in a writing class who doesn't write is a fraud.

I used fear as fuel.

I wrote that night and the night after that. And I wrote until I finished my first story. It was terrible. The instructor told me this later on, but it didn't matter.

I had taken the first step towards facing my fears.

I don't recall one moment where I conquered my fears though. Instead, I got a job as a journalist writing for a newspaper.

There, I had to finish my articles by a deadline because if I didn't the editor would fire me.

I know this because he called me into his office after I missed a deadline and told me.

I was more afraid of the unemployment line than reaching the end.

So I stopped polishing my articles until they were perfect and started finishing them. On more than one occasion, my editor sent the articles back to me saying I'd left out an important paragraph or that my introduction needed reworking.

This criticism made me want to quit.

On other occasions, the subeditors of the paper reworked my article entirely. Having my work taken apart like that felt like an interrogation, but at least I was getting paid to write.

I still struggle with fear today.

While writing this book I was afraid others would ask, "What right do you have to explain how to be productive?"

I still think that.

I also knew I'd spent hours researching productivity methods and studying how artists work. I'd read dozens of books by authors explaining how they work.

I knew enough to organise my thoughts into a book. Although I am nobody, I gave myself permission to write a book because writers must start somewhere.

Even if feels terrifying.

I don't like personal writing like this. It's hard work, and it reveals more of me than a guide to the writing tools I use. I almost deleted this chapter several times before I hit publish.

What's to enjoy about revealing a job didn't work out, that I was lazy and that my work failed?

Stephen Pressfield made me do it.

In *The War of Art*, he said, "Write with the door closed, rewrite with the door open."

Are you paralyzed with fear? That's a good sign. Fear is good. Like self-doubt, fear is an indicator. Fear tells us what we have to do. Remember one rule of thumb: the more scared we are of a work or calling, the more sure we can be that we have to do it.

PRESS FORWARDS

Give yourself permission to start and make messy mistakes.

Remind yourself everyone who wants to become a successful writer must start somewhere and now is your time. Once you begin, you're already ahead of the writer who said, "No, not today. I'm not ready."

Spend more time creating than consuming. You already know more than enough and, like a snowballing rolling downhill, you just need a little momentum.

If you're having trouble finishing your work, set artificial deadlines and stick to them.

When the time comes and even if your work isn't quite ready, show it to a group of people you trust like a writing group. Ask for their help. Then go and fix your writing.

As you get into the habit of finishing your work, you will win more opportunities to gain feedback.

Later, show the world what you created. Enter contests and submit your articles to magazines or websites. Let them judge it in all its ugly imperfections. Respond if you need to or move on. Judgment is better than being ignored.

Anne Frank wrote her autobiography when she was just 15.

Helen Keller wrote the story of her Life at aged 22.

Franz Kafka finished his first novel in his twenties.

Christy Brown used what he lacked as fuel for his books rather than as excuses not to write. (See chapter 12).

Charles Bukowski wrote in obscurity for much of his life, until the publication of his novel *Post Office*, when he was 51.

These are extreme examples.

I'm an extreme kind of person.

Are you?

WRITE IN THE FACE OF FEAR

I was rejected three times while writing this chapter. I contacted five authors I admire with interview requests.

Four of them said no. I asked several podcasting experts to share their advice for a guest blog post. Half of them didn't reply. I pitched guest posts at the editors of three big blogs, two of whom said no.

These rejections are tough, but they are normal experiences for the productive writer.

If you want to become a more productive writer, rejection waits for you at the beginning, in the middle and at the end of your work.

Everybody who succeeds gets rejected at some point during their careers.

By turning up and creating, you cut through your fears. Even if some people reject your work, others will embrace it. The next website you pitch might accept your ideas. Your next interview request might be granted.

You must write today. You must write now. You must write like your life depends on it.

Because it does.

USE PROVEN FORMULAS

"Always enter the conversation already occurring in the customer's mind." – Dan S. Kennedy

Copywriting is writing that sells a product or service.

If the reader is unconvinced by the last paragraph, or if they don't read that far, the copywriter has failed.

Great copywriting captures the readers' attention and persuades them to take action. It convinces them to buy or sign up.

As a writer, you might not always be persuading your reader to buy a product or service, but you certainly are persuading them to do something.

You want them to give you their attention, believe that your ideas hold value and take action on your advice.

Copywriting excels at this kind of persuasion. And while great copywriting is part art, the highly persuasive writing on countless billboards, magazine advertisements and online marketing campaigns is driven by tried and tested formulas that have worked for decades.

BRYAN COLLINS

If you learn copywriting, you will learn how to sell with your words and find the success your writing deserves.

The copywriting formulas in this chapter will help you master the basics faster.

HOW TO USE PAS FORMULA

The simplest and most effective copywriting solution is the Problem-Agitate-Solution Formula or PAS. Copywriters have used this for years to put food on the table because it works.

Let's break down this three-part formula:

- **Problem**: Offer a problem the reader is experiencing.
- **Agitate:** Use emotional language to intensify the problem.
- **Solution**: Provide a credible solution to the problem.

New writers who start a blog often complain about a lack of website traffic. As a result they feel frustrated and anxious about how they're spending their blogging time. Let's tackle this problem for these new writers and illustrate this formula.

[Problem]

Are you sick and tired of writing articles and blog posts that nobody reads?

Now let's whip up our reader's emotions:

[Agitate]

Millions of aspiring writers just like you publish posts every day, worry about SEO and wonder if they should spend hundreds of dollars advertising on Facebook.

But unless you spend your time in the right places, you're

never going to build the kind of audience you need to grow a successful blog.

Now we offer the reader a lifeline:

[Solution]

What if I told you there's a better way? What if I told you guest blogging could help you attract thousands of new readers?

See how this formula uses a problem to draw the reader in?

HOW TO USE THE APPROACH FORMULA

Copywriters adapted this approach from a template often used by door-to-door salesmen. It's a soft sell where the writer works hard to make the right initial impression on the reader. You can easily learn this six-part formula.

- Arrive
- Propose
- Persuade
- Reassure
- Make an offer
- Ask for the order

To use the Approach Formula, say something the reader will agree with – something non-threatening that shows you're both on the same page. Then, propose a course of action, something most people who agree with the arriving statement would find reasonable.

Next, gently persuade the reader that this course of action is the correct one. Finally, reassure the reader by over-coming any possible objections. Below, I've used this formula to convince new writers that they can master their chosen craft if they know where to start.

[Arrive]

Becoming a great writer doesn't happen overnight.

[Propose]

You know there's no quick fix or great secret to writing mastery. It simply takes practice. In fact, in his popular book *Outliers*, Malcolm Gladwell suggests a person must commit to 10,000 hours of practice to master a craft. But unguided practice is a terribly inefficient way to learn. That's why it could be time for you to hire a coach.

[Persuade]

A writing coach will allow you to combine practice with the experienced feedback necessary to hone your skills in the fastest possible time. A writing coach will guide you past obstacles that will block you for hours, days or weeks working alone.

[Reassure]

But if engaging a writing coach sounds complicated and expensive, don't worry—I'm going to keep this simple. I'll share the five things new writers should look for in a coach. I'll even show you how to get coaching for free.

New writers who are ready to get help should look for five things from their next writing coach.

(Now the copywriter should go into specifics about what to expect from a good writing coach).

[Make an Offer-Ask for the Order]

If you need help with writing, it's time to act. We'll spend three months working one-on-one, so you can finally go from the first page to the last page. There's just one problem: places are limited.

Sign up now.

SELL YOUR PRODUCT OR SERVICE

Whatever you're selling, you must be able to tell a compelling story about your product or service and how it's going to improve the lives of customers.

Even if you're writing copy for a boring product or service, you can still bring a sense of passion or excitement to a salespage.

Famous copywriter David Ogilvy wrote about the Rolls-Royce, "At 60 miles an hour the loudest noise in this new Rolls-Royce comes from the electric clock."

What's compelling about this example is Ogilvy's use of small details to bring this statement to life. He puts the reader right in the car.

Here's another example:

Taking piano classes isn't the most glamorous way to pass time, but in 1926, John Caples wrote one of the most famous advertorials of all time about piano classes for the U.S. School of Music.

The headline for his famous advertorial reads, "They Laughed When I Sat Down At the Piano But When I Started to Play!"

Caples goes on to describe how, thanks to a course by the U.S. School of Music, he surprised his friends and family by playing the piano.

> I played on and as I played I forgot the people around me. I forgot the hour, the place, the breathless listeners. The little world I lived in seemed to fade—seemed to grow dim— unreal. Only the music was real.

This advertorial blurs the line between art and copy. This ad isn't just about learning to play the piano; it's about the power of music and how we all aspire to become better people.

Caples's ad also demonstrates how a copywriter can use an emotional benefit of a product or service, tell a story and win over customers and readers.

Whether you're writing about consumer electronics, sports cars or a more boring product like an insurance product, the basics remain the same.

GRAB THEM BY THE EYEBALLS

Your readers and customers won't click on boring, bland or unsexy headlines.

So grab them by the eyeballs with an engaging headline.

If you're struggling to find a good headline for your article, take a look at magazine covers like *Cosmopolitan*.

The writers for magazines like *Cosmopolitan* are well-paid pros, and you can easily rework any of these proven headlines to suit your copywriting.

For example, I recently found the *Cosmopolitan* headline "10 Sex Myths Busted!" and turned it into "10 Writing Myths Busted!" and I used the latter for a blog post. (See chapter 19).

Write at least 10 headlines for every article, salespage or book chapter you write and you will get better at the art of headline writing.

USE EVERYDAY LANGUAGE

Author and salesperson Dan Kennedy best explains why words that sells must be simple and easy to read.

"I think sales letters should be reader-friendly. That means the letter appears easy to read, is easy on the eye, uses everyday language, and doesn't require you to be a Harvard grad or a determined masochist to get through it," he wote in *The Ultimate Sales Letter.*

I think of this sentence every time I pick up an indecipherable pamphlet from the insurance company, a jargon letter from the bank or a detailed brochure from my electricity provider.

Most of the time these documents are impossible to read, and they almost always end up in the bin.

The next time you write copy for your audience consider if you use use everyday language.

ACTIVATE YOUR VERBS

One of the best ways to give your copy about a product or service more life is to shun the passive voice in favour of the active voice.

In the passive voice, the subject (you) is acted on by a verb. It sounds weak, and you can usually spot the passive voice if a verb ends with -ed.

For example:

- It was decided . . .
- The product was revealed . . .
- A product is going to be . . .

In the active voice, the subject (you) performs the action. For example:

- We're releasing . . .
- We're announcing . . .
- We've just updated . . .

I'll cover the active voice in more detail in chapter 31. However, if you're writing copy, remember the active voice will help your writing sparkle and capture your readers' (or customers') attention.

INCLUDE A CALL-TO-ACTION

When you finish your copy, always call on your readers to act.

You could say:

- If you enjoyed this post, share it on Facebook/Twitter/LinkedIn.
- Share your tips for [insert topic] in the comments sections.
- Watch this free video/download this free resource to learn more about [insert topic here].
- Join the Insider list and get exclusive tips for [insert benefit here].
- Begin your 30-day free trial of [insert product] here.

SELL LIKE A PRO

Copywriting is a skill like any other, and you've got to practice to improve. You can use the PAS or Approach formulas to sell products, ideas and services to your readers.

I recommend saving great examples of copy in your personal file so you can see what works.

If you make a habit of writing copy and studying how the experts sell with words, you'll naturally discover what sells and what doesn't work.

You'll become the kind of productive writer who knows how to build lasting relationships with readers and customers.

SELL WITH POWER WORDS

Below, I've provided fifty top power words which many marketers and copywriters use. These words will help you invoke emotion in the reader and accomplish more with your writing or sales copy.

- Agony
- Astonishing
- Announcing
- Alert
- Beware
- Confidential
- Compare
- Devoted
- Download
- Evil
- Excited
- Extra
- Fearless
- Fortune
- Free
- Fulfil
- Genuine
- Gift
- Growth
- Guaranteed
- Happy
- Hero
- Insider
- Introducing
- Immediate
- Improved
- Important

- Jail
- Mind-blowing
- New
- Obsession
- Practical
- Private
- Prize
- Refundable
- Sale
- Security
- Sex
- Silly
- Strange
- Slaughter
- Sleazy
- Strong
- Tax
- Urgent
- Ultimate
- Unusual
- Valuable
- Zero

There are hundreds more power words like these.

If you write online, use Twitter to research the power words that work best for your ideas. You can do this by tweeting different headlines to the same piece of writing several hours apart and determining which headlines perform best.

If you don't have a large Twitter following, study the most popular social media posts and blogs in your industry and take note of the emotional words writers use in their headlines.

I also recommend visiting BuzzFeed. The headline

writers of this popular entertainment and news website are masters of using power words and emotional language to encourage more people to click on their headlines.

Whatever your approach, a swipe file is an ideal place to store power words that work for you. It will save you hours of writing time.

KNOW WHAT YOU'RE WRITING ABOUT

"We may be very busy, we may be very efficient, but we will also be truly effective only when we begin with the end in mind." – Stephen R. Covey

The productive writer understands great writing does at least one of four things. It informs, educates, inspires or entertains readers.

A news story is informative because it tells the reader something important about a current event. A tutorial is educational because it explains to readers how to accomplish a task.

A short story is entertaining because it gives the reader a place to escape their troubles. A self-help book is inspirational because it shows readers how they can improve their lives.

Before you start writing, decide if you want to entertain, inform, educate or inspire your reader. You don't have to achieve all four, but your writing should tick at least one of these boxes. If you don't, your reader will lose interest in your writing.

The good news is, you can easily give your readers what they want and hold their attention.

HOW TO INFORM YOUR READERS

Informing your readers means peppering your writing with research and facts that build credibility.

If you're writing for a publication, your editor will provide clear directions about what your writing should achieve and how you can give your readers what they want.

When I worked as a freelance journalist, I often received detailed briefs from editors explaining the topic I should cover, whom I should interview and how long the piece should be.

Even if you're not working for an editor, consider yourself a journalist who must examine a single topic with an unblinking gaze. You must be clear and level-headed in your writing.

You must put some distance between your feelings and the facts. Informative writing means you'll be spending time interviewing experts and finding unusual facts and information of interest to your readers.

HOW TO EDUCATE YOUR READERS

Educating your reader means adopting a personal and helpful tone. Put your hand around your reader's shoulder and say, "This isn't so hard to achieve. I can help you."

Examples of educational writing include tutorials, step-by-step articles, how-to guides and this book chapter.

You don't have to be an expert to educate your readers either.

Consider the curious case of the teenage maths student struggling with a difficult equation. Instead of asking the teacher for advice, he turns to his friend and asks him how to solve the equation.

In this case, the teenage maths student feels more comfortable asking his friend for advice because he can relate to his friend. This is because the two of them are at similar points along their learning journeys. You can use this principle to relate to your readers even if you're not an expert.

For example, in 2014 I ran the Dublin City marathon. It was my first marathon. I'm not an expert at running or athletics and I would never profess to be.

However, I could draw on the mistakes I made while training for this marathon to write an article like, "Marathon Training Mistakes: 10 Lessons for Beginners".

My beginner's article wouldn't interest serious runners, but a beginner considering their first race might be more interested in what I learnt because we're not so different. If you are going to write an educational article you want people to relate to, use clear and simple instructions the reader can follow.

If you've ever read the instruction manual for an old appliance, you will appreciate how frustrating ambiguous instructions are.

You should also provide practical tips free of jargon or opinion. This way, the reader can learn from your knowledge and decide for themselves what to do next.

Using metaphors the reader relates to will improve your writing too. A metaphor is a clever way of relating a concept to an everyday object or action.

For example, "Running a blog is a lot like servicing a car because…" or "Writing a book is a lot like laying bricks because…"

Finally, encourage the reader to persevere when they feel like giving up. Remind the reader you were a beginner once too, and then show them what success looks like.

HOW TO INSPIRE YOUR READERS

Inspiring readers is a different job. Often, this means drawing on personal stories and passions. You must invoke an emotion or change in your readers. You should persuade them to act and push them over the edge if they don't.

To inspire, consider what they should feel after reading your work or what they should take away from your writing. Play on their fears and hopes.

Paint a version of hell that they should avoid or describe a vision of the future as you see it. Give your readers specific examples of how you both can move towards your version of heaven together.

The most famous example of inspirational writing is Martin Luther King Jr's "I have a Dream speech", within which he paints his dream "that my four little children will one day live in a nation where they will not be judged by the colour of their skin but by the content of their character."

HOW TO ENTERTAIN YOUR READERS

Entertaining the reader means drawing on personal stories only you can tell.

Yes, you can use humour, anecdotes, and clever wordplay, but story is king. We make sense of the world through story-telling and turn to this medium as an escape.

The best way to entertain your readers is to tell a captivating story. There are entire books about effective story-telling, and I recommend reading *Story* by Robert McKee.

If you want to learn about story faster, one of the simplest and best storytelling concepts is this six sentence fill-in-the-blanks template created by Pixar Studios, which they outline on their blog.

Once upon a time there was . . . Every day . . . One day . . . Because of that . . . Because of that . . . Until finally . . .

Here's how this storytelling template works for the popular animated Pixar film *Finding Nemo*:

Once upon a time there was . . . a widowed fish, named Marlin, who was extremely protective of his only son, Nemo. Every day . . . Marlin warned Nemo of the ocean's dangers and implored him not to swim far away. One day . . . in an act of defiance, Nemo ignored his father's warnings and swam into the open water.

Because of that . . . he was captured by a diver and ended up in the fish tank of a dentist in Sydney. Because of that . . . Marlin set off on a journey to recover Nemo, enlisting the help of other sea creatures along the way. Until finally . . . Marlin and Nemo found each other, reunite and learned that love depends on trust.

How about this?

Once upon a time there was a new writer who couldn't finish what he started. Every day, he tried to write but kept getting distracted. One day, his editor boss fired him because he wasn't able to ship his work on time. Because of that the writer almost went broke. Because of that, he taught himself how to find better paying freelance contracts and get more things done. Until finally he made a habit of finishing what he started and got paid for his hard work.

BEGIN WITH YOUR READERS IN MIND

The writer who starts a project without knowing what they want to accomplish will find their work hard, slow and awkward.

Deciding the purpose of your work or beginning with the end in mind before you put words onto the blank page will give confines within which to write. It will give you a goal to write towards and help you finish what you started.

Remember, most readers are hungry for information and for a perspective that only YOU have.

If you want to become a more productive writer, give it to them.

STOP SEARCHING FOR THE PERFECT WRITING TOOL

"Do not wait; the time will never be 'just right'. Start where you stand, and work with whatever tools you may have at your command, and better tools will be found as you go along." – George Herbert

The productive writer knows the perfect writing tool doesn't exist. He or she spends most of their time trying to hit their target word count for the day and improve their craft.

He or she has their quirks too.

Hemingway wrote drafts of his works standing up with a pencil and paper.

Lewis Carroll declined a chair in favour of standing while writing.

Vladimir Nabokov, the Russian-American author of *Lolita,* wrote drafts of his novels on index cards and gave them to his wife to organise.

Every accomplished writer has a routine and idiosyncrasies. Writing while standing up might have worked for Hemingway and using index cards might have worked for

Nabokov, but that doesn't mean these tools are suitable for you.

By all means, study how the greats completed their works, but don't let your search for the perfect writing tool (or a novel approach to writing) get in the way of producing more words. Doing the work and mastering your craft is more important than learning how to use the latest writing tool.

For years, I was obsessed with finding the perfect writing tool.

I told myself things like:

"When I get this piece of software, I'll be able to write more often."

"This computer is the one I'm going to finally write a book with."

"I need to learn how to use this piece of software before I write a book."

Just as a bad tradesman blames their tools when they botch a job, a bad writer blames his or her tools when they can't finish what they started.

ON NEW WRITING TOOLS

I'm no Luddite.

Sometimes, the productive writer sets time aside to learn how to use a new writing tool.

Scrivener, for example, is a powerful piece of writing software that's popular with many writers today.

This application has a small learning curve, but it simplifies working on different parts of your book. Scrivener also enables you to manipulate the structure of whatever you're writing and compile different versions for book stores, websites and more.

Similarly, many writers can skyrocket their word count

through dictation software. Again, they have to invest some time in mastering dictation and then incorporate this new way of writing into their creative workflow

However, a productive writer sets time aside to master a new tool after they've completed the day's work. Later, he or she masters this new tool by using it.

The procrastinating writer, on the other hand, puts off doing their most important work because they want to learn how to use every feature in their new tool of choice. He or she spends hours setting up this new tool so that everything is perfect when it's finally time to write.

ON WRITING WITH A COMPUTER

Computers enable more productive writing. It's quicker to manipulate large blocks of text on screen than on paper, and you stand less chance of losing your work.

That said, computers are far from perfect. The blink of the cursor and the lure of distractions like email, social media and the internet place boundaries around a writer's creativity and productivity.

Some writers find computers confining. Steven Pressfield, author of *The War of Art*, prefers writing on his Smith-Corona typewriter over a computer, for example.

If you're having problems working a piece out, try writing for 30 minutes with pen and paper before returning to your computer. I've found this method forces me to write slower and stay with a thought longer.

It's also a good idea to work on early drafts of your work on pen and paper or with index cards and move to a computer for later drafts.

Find and use what works, and accept it in all its imperfections.

ON THE INTERNET

During a book tour for his 2012 novel *Freedom*, American novelist Jonathan Franzen told a journalist he wanted to write more each day, so he physically removed his Wi-Fi card from his computer and permanently blocked his machine's Ethernet connection with super glue.

I'm not suggesting you wreck your machine or that an internet-free life is the path to becoming a *New York Times* best-selling author. But disabling your internet access, even for short periods, will help you accomplish more on the page.

Think of your internet-free writing sessions as a respite from the deluge of information you wade through every day.

If you need to use the internet for research, try to wait until after you've hit your target word count for the day.

I've never written anything of consequence while navigating from one site to the next. The internet comes with too many distractions, feeds, unchecked emails, pings and notifications.

The blank page doesn't stand a chance in the face of a digital crowd clamouring for our attention.

Writing off-line can feel liberating and intimate. You won't feel a subconscious tug to log into an account or refresh a feed.

It's just you, your words and your ideas.

ON TIDYING UP

A master craftsman tidies up after themselves and prepares their work for the following day. He knows creativity is a long-term game and to turn up and do the work.

Hemingway, for example, stopped writing in the middle

of a sentence so he'd know where to resume the following day.

You don't need to follow his approach. Just have a clear idea of what you're going to write tomorrow.

Perhaps you want to finish your introduction, expand on a chapter in your book, or work on an outline?

Tidy up your work, organise your notes and put your tools away. Tip the waitress in the coffee shop if you need to. Make it easier to find the clear space you need to write again tomorrow and improve your craft.

EMBRACE STRUCTURE

"I fear those big words which make us so unhappy" – James Joyce

Do you want to know how to organise your writing?

If you do, planning and structure are your new best friends.

Finishing a writing project is easier, and readers will enjoy your work more if it's supported by an underlying structure. This is why books have paragraphs, chapters and narrative arcs.

It's why blog posts have subheadings and newspaper articles are broken up with pull quotes, panels and boxes. Even the directors and writers of most successful films break them into three acts.

PLAN AHEAD

Several years ago, I had to write a these longer than 20,000 words about the literary works of Irish author Christy Brown.

For months, I struggled with this thesis. I just couldn't get it to flow, and I couldn't organise my ideas. I told my tutor I was afraid I wouldn't be able to finish my work. She asked, "Why don't you approach your thesis from a different angle? Why don't you outline it?"

I took my tutor's advice and developed an outline of each section and chapter using pen and paper. I wrote down the title of each chapter on almost one hundred 6x4 index cards. (3x5 and 5x8 cards are good too!)

Next, I wrote down points I wanted to cover within each chapter along with quotes, stories and other pieces of factual information. I laid my index cards out on a large glass table and spent several hours reviewing them.

What happened next surprised me.

I was able to shift from one troublesome section or chapter to an easier one without getting lost or stressed. I could see the overall structure of my thesis even if it was unfinished. In effect, I zoomed out from my thesis and moved the chapters and ideas around like the pieces on a chessboard.

I considered where I was repeating myself, what was missing and what I needed to cover. Then, I sorted the index cards into piles to keep, remove or combine. Next I rewrote each of the index cards and repeated this planning process.

I did this until I was left with a structure for my thesis that I could work with. Although the thesis changed during the course of writing and rewriting, this structure served as a light that kept me from getting lost during the creative process.

REDUCE, REMOVE AND SIMPLIFY

Confession: I hate shopping for clothes. It's time-consuming, draining, and I'm terrible at it.

I never know what to buy, and I always think there's a better choice just around the corner.

One hot summer's day, I had to buy a shirt and tie for a wedding. I spent several hours walking from suit shop to suit shop in Dublin and trying on clothes I didn't like.

I was sweaty, tired and about to give up my search and go home. Then I decided to try an airy and quiet shop near the bus stop.

When I walked inside, the owner took one look at me and pulled out a chair.

"You look like a man who needs a seat," he said. "How can I help you?"

I explained my predicament.

"I just don't know what I want. There's so much out there."

"What do you like? What are you looking for?" he asked.

While I explained, he laid out three shirts and ties on the table.

"Try these three on."

"Why only three?" I asked pointing to all the other suits and ties behind us.

"I never give a customer too much choice," he said. "It makes decisions harder."

He was right. I found selecting from his three choices much easier than considering the hundreds of other choices in the shop.

SIMPLIFY YOUR WRITING

Business writer and online entrepreneur Chris Brogan best sums the benefits of simplification.

He told writer and podcaster James Altucher in a 2014 interview, "The sun can warm an entire field of daisies, or you can focus it such that it can burn through an inch of steel."

Focus on the heart of your writing and cut anything that doesn't add value. If you're struggling to simplify your writing, consider:

- What angles and points can you combine or remove?
- Are you being too technical?
- What should your writing focus on?
- What should it ignore?
- Can you sum up your topic in one sentence?
- If not, what's preventing you from doing so?
- How can you use fewer words?

HOW I SIMPLIFY MY WRITING

When I'm writing feature articles, I reduce the number of interviewees I quote because too many interviewees can become confusing for the reader. This reduction also lends greater weight to the included interviewees, and it gives me room to analyse what they said.

While writing this book, I simplified my work by reducing what I've discovered about productivity into 33 digestible strategies. I did this because 33 strategies was the best way to reduce my idea to the essentials.

When I'm writing a blog post, I pick an idea and consider people who will want to read about it. I ask what new perspective or information I can add to this topic and how I can solve a problem for readers.

I make room for an introduction and conclusion and also for some factual information, personal anecdotes and stories from my commonplace book. Then I write a rough first draft somewhere between 1000 and 1,500 words.

Later, I reread this first draft and consider what I should remove and rework. I check if my sentences are too long and if I can break up paragraphs into a list. Online readers spend more time scanning than reading articles, so I must ensure my writing is easy on the eye.

PLAN TO WRITE, PLAN TO FINISH

Authors like James Joyce and Samuel Beckett wrote without planning or structure, but they still learnt what structure was before abandoning it.

Next time you are faced with an intimidating writing project, break it into chunks that you can tackle one by one. On index cards, jot down words identifying these chunks, and then rearrange these in order of how your writing project unfolds.

This process will give you an early overview of your writing project. This planning will also help you zoom out and see all the pieces on your chessboard. From there, you can create a structure that works for you.

Your writing will evolve during the creative process, but having a plan and using structure can help you get from the blank page to the last page.

WRITE WITH A BEGINNER'S MIND

"When you do something, you should burn yourself completely, like a good bonfire, leaving no trace of yourself." – Shunryu Suzuki

So you're an expert.

You know how to organise your ideas, you've put in your 10,000 hours of dedicated practice, and you know how to write.

But can you still write as if you are considering an idea for the first time?

Shunryu Suzuki was a twentieth-century Japanese Zen monk and teacher who authored *Zen Mind, Beginner's Mind*.

In this book of Zen teachings and talks, Suzuki writes that when we are intentional in our practice, we act, or write, without bias or preconceptions. Instead, when the task at hand consumes us completely.

To take on a task, and know how it will turn out beforehand is to hold something back from the creative fire.

To bring your preconceptions and biases is to forget the

perspective of those who know less than you. Instead, put everything you know into the fire of the creative process and let it burn.

- Perhaps the argument you set out to prove isn't as solid as you thought.
- Maybe a character in your story wants to do something that you didn't expect.
- Possibly your research unearths a new angle or story for your work.

If you're an expert, this open-minded approach to writing is hard to take.

When you become practised at a task or skill, your writing voice dulls itself on a groove of repetition. Your arguments establish themselves and opinions solidify before the fire of your hard work takes hold.

You turn to the same haggard metaphors and imagery and drag them out long after their prime.

You fail to see things from the point of view of your less informed readers, and you miss those interesting detours that form part of the creative process.

Remember, a reader will get more from the writer who feels passionate about his or her subject.

USE THE OUTSIDER'S PERSPECTIVE

Consider starting a new job.

For the first few weeks or months, you are an outsider who sees the workplace differently from the rest of the team. Even if you keep your questions to yourself, you wonder why things are done one way and not the other.

In the beginning, you are a unique commodity and sometimes forward-thinking managers will capitalise on your outsider's insight to make informed changes. They know you can see things the rest of the team can't.

When these first few weeks turn into months or years, you will acquire expert knowledge about your company or workplace. You will become the kind of person who does things a certain way because that's how it's always been done.

Your expert knowledge, experiences and insight about a topic or field of study can induce complacency.

How can you write something original when the tinder wood of your creativity is soaked with preconceptions? How many times have you made the same moot point? Have you become an insider?

If the facts change, abandon your arguments. Don't become too attached to any one idea or way of accomplishing things on the blank page.

If you get the chance, leave your old arguments behind and don't look back.

CHANGE YOUR MIND

Writing with a beginner's mind means bringing a renewed sense of curiosity to your project.

Seek out new answers in place of old ones you take for granted.

Evaluate your ideas like you've come across them for the first time.

Throw rocks at your arguments and see if they still hold up.

Accept some of your readers will know things you don't.

Acknowledge your mistakes. But what if you're worried about being inconsistent or what others will think?

You can get away with changing your mind if you take readers on a journey with you. Your loyal readers will forgive you for an about-turn if you explain why you changed your mind. If they don't, at least you had the courage to state what you know is true.

Your readers might thank you for it... later.

QUESTION OLD ASSUMPTIONS

At first, Italian astronomer Galileo Galilei believed the world was the flat centre of the universe like his scientific peers. Then in 1616, after stumbling across new facts with his telescope, he presented his change of mind to an unready Italian audience.

He argued why the world is round.

Although the Church didn't forgive him while he was alive for this "heresy", today we regard Galileo as one of humanity's top polymaths.

Early in life, British author George Orwell believed strongly in the entitlements of the upper class. Later in life, he satirised them in his dystopian novel *1984*. He wrote, "Orthodoxy means not thinking–not needing to think. Orthodoxy is unconsciousness."

Author Leo Tolstoy was a staunch follower of the Russian Orthodox and a man who believed keeping serfs was acceptable.

Later, he explained why he abandoned his old principles in his short book *A Confession*.

> I cannot recall those years without horror, loathing, and heart-rending pain. I killed people in war, challenged men to duels with the purpose of killing them, and lost at cards; I squandered the fruits of the peasants' toil and then had them executed; I was a fornicator and a cheat. Lying, stealing, promiscuity of every kind, drunkenness, violence, murder — there was not a crime I did not commit... Thus I lived for ten years.

You might not have committed a crime, duelled with your fellow man or lost at cards like Tolstoy, but when you look back on the years past, what have you changed your mind about?

Now, write about it.

BURN UP WITH YOUR READER

Hold out your hand to your readers and invite them on a journey that you have never taken together.

Show your reader why your idea warrants his or her attention. Reveal the mistakes you've made, the times you fell down, the lessons you learned and what your world looks like today.

Practice writing from this beginner's mind until you can approach the blank page without any preconceived notions.

Write like you're experiencing something for the first time. Write like it's you and the reader against the world, and together you will burn like a good bonfire.

DON'T STOP EXPERIMENTING

"Every person takes the limits of their own field of vision for the limits of the world." – Arthur Schopenhauer

Roald Dahl found success by experimenting with elements from his life on the blank page.

As a young man, he worked for Shell in Kenya and Tanzania and spent his free time hunting. During World War II, Dahl became a decorated fighter ace and intelligence officer.

He shot down at least two enemy JU-88 planes, took part in the Battle of Athens and was one of the last pilots to withdraw from Greece during the German invasion.

When he became a writer, Dahl wasn't afraid to draw on his old life for his new creative one. He wrote several short stories about his time as a fighter pilot and in his novels and short stories drew extensively on his previous careers.

For example, in *James and the Giant Peach*, the seagulls (or fighter airplanes) attack the airborne giant peach, a talking centipede falls (or parachutes) off the giant peach, and the end of the book references air raids and heroes returning home (from the war).

Even though he first became famous as the author of children's books like *The BFG* and *Charlie and the Chocolate Factory*. Dahl refused to be pigeonholed into one genre or towards catering to a particular audience. He wrote poetry, published screenplays and became a successful adult short story writer.

The embodiment of a productive writer, Dahl wrote more than 17 stories for children, two novels and series of short story collections.

He was a consummate scientist of his craft.

ACCEPT SOME LIMITATIONS

Before you experiment, consider what's possible with the written word. This medium engages only two to three of the five human senses: sight, touch, sound, taste and smell.

The reader can see your words on the page, but when you describe someone's face, the reader must use their imagination to fill in the blanks.

They can feel the weight and texture of the paper in their hands, but when you write about the texture of someone's skin, they bring their biases to your writing.

If you describe the bitter taste of a coffee, the reader's sense of taste and smell are just as likely to be triggered by the environment where they're reading your writing.

There are exceptions.

Poetry read aloud is musical to the ear. You can also use onomatopoeia or words that sound like their meaning – such as cuckoo or sizzle – to engage your reader's senses.

Today many writers read their works aloud at public events or in the form of audio books.

The productive writer sometimes uses picture, video and audio to convey his or her message. He knows alternative media complements fine writing.

He makes lengthy passages destined for the computer screen more digestible by breaking them up with bullet points, headings, pull quotes and the clever use of **bold** and *italics* formatting.

This is particularly true if you're writing for online readers who are just as likely to listen to an audio clip or watch a video as they are to read a blog post.

LEARN TO EXPERIMENT

Have you ever read my erotic fiction?

I'm embarrassed to tell you this, but several years ago I researched what was popular and trending, and I tried to write several different erotic short stories.

My creative experiment blew up in my face.

I discovered erotic fiction is exceptionally difficult to write without coming across as clichéd or sleazy. My stories came across as both.

I never published my stories, and I discovered I don't have the talent or desire to write the next *Fifty Shades of Grey*. Thankfully, my humiliation was a private one, an experiment that helped me find the limitations of my craft.

I realised I preferred writing non-fiction.

The best way to discover the limitations of your craft is to explore what works and what doesn't work for you. Find what excites and bores you.

Take on new creative and writing challenges. Through brave experimentation, you will figure out the rules of writing and discover the ones that are OK to bend and the ones you should snap in half.

If writers didn't take time to experiment with their craft,

we wouldn't have books like *Ulysses* or *The Dubliners*. James Joyce is an extreme example, but aspiring writers can learn from the working habits of the greats.

For you, this might mean writing poetry, a novel, a short story or a personal essay. It means getting out of your creative comfort zone.

- If you've written a story in the first person, rewrite it in the third person.
- If you've written a blog post about the benefits of meditation, turn it into 50 reasons why meditation is better than sex.
- If you opened your article with a statistic, use a quote or a statement that will rile your reader.
- If you've just finished an article, remove the introduction and insert the conclusion in its place.
- If you tried to be impartial, rewrite your work using a strong, personal point of view.

GET RESULTS

Experimenting is time-consuming, and you're going to make mistakes. But nobody has to see them. And the more you make, the better writer you will become.

Dahl said, "A little nonsense now and then, is relished by the wisest men."

So aim for a little nonsense.

Experiment, just like I did by writing awful erotic fiction.

The hard work, the mistakes, failed experiments, and torn-up manuscripts – these activities form 90 percent of what is not seen, like an iceberg under water.

But…

These private little experiments are a great way to

develop your writing voice and push your boundaries beyond what you feel most comfortable doing.

At the least, you're less likely to become bored with your craft and more excited about the possibilities of the blank page.

BUILD YOUR PLATFORM

"Compared to the cost of renting eyeballs, buying a platform is cheap." – Seth Godin

David doesn't like marketing his writing. He says his job is to write, not to promote his work. That if he works hard enough on his art, then his readers will come.

But only a few people have come across David's work. And when they do, they don't stay long.

Sound familiar?

Not too long ago, I was David. And if you're a writer struggling to find an audience for your work online, he's you too.

Writing is a hard, demanding craft, and nothing is more disappointing than releasing your work into a vacuum.

You can overcome these problems by building a platform for your work.

BUILD A PLATFORM

The gatekeepers between you and your audience no longer exist. Today, you can create opportunities that were unavailable when writers like John Cheever, Virginia Woolf and Stephen King started out.

You need a platform to tell stories about yourself, showcase your work and find readers.

Your platform should comprise a blog or author website, an email list and a preferred social media channel. The goal of your platform is to provide people with a way to discover you and give you a way to talk to your readers.

Many authors today use social media to connect with readers. Brazilian novelist Paulo Coelho has an astonishing 10 million followers on Twitter (@paulocoelho). Neil Gaiman is also an avid user of Twitter (@neilhimself) and blogs at journal.neilgaiman.com.

However, Facebook and Twitter are outposts that you have little control over. When they change the rules (as they often do), you can't do much about it.

For this reason, you should have full control over your website. It's your home base and the number one place readers can find you. At the least, your website should explain who you are, what you write about and how people can get in touch. You can showcase your books too.

After you've set up your website, create an email list and ask readers to join by offering a free book or some of your best writing.

Having an email list is helpful for communicating directly with readers or customers, particularly if Amazon or Twitter changes the rules. Plus, you'll be less dependent on search engines for traffic and readers. You can ask loyal email subscribers for feedback on early drafts too.

Finally, blogging is a great outlet for non-fiction writers.

You can experiment with different writing styles. Writing blog posts gets you into the habit of presenting your work to more than your spouse, family member or best friend.

WRITE GUEST BLOG POSTS

I used to resent the idea of spending time and energy writing blog posts and then giving them away for free. Surely I was better off publishing posts on my site?

I was dead wrong.

My personal blogging mentor, Jon Morrow, said writing guest posts for large websites is the writer's equivalent of opening for the Rolling Stones when you're an up-and-coming band.

It's the quickest way to grow your audience.

When you write for a large website, a new audience will read your work and potentially visit your site and join your email list.

If you write several successful guest blog posts, ask the site owners to share your writing or promote your book. This is cheaper and more efficient than trying to run an advertising campaign.

Also when an editor reviews your posts, you'll receive feedback that will help you improve at your craft. Many new writers pay for this kind of constructive feedback.

As a productive writer, you can make peace with this marketing strategy because it allows you to write, promote your work and get editorial feedback.

WRITE LIKE CHARLES BUKOWSKI

In his famous collection of poetry *The Pleasures of the Damned*, Charles Bukowski complained about how his heroes (Hemingway, F. Scott Fitzgerald) could find an audience for their work easier in the 1920s than he could in the 1940s and 1950s.

> It was much easier to be a genius in the twenties, there were only 3 or 4 literary magazines.... you could possibly meet Picasso for a glass of wine.

Bukowski then bemoaned the number of publications he had to deal with to build his audience in 1951.

I wonder how Bukowski would have embraced the millions of websites, blogs, and publications today's writers contend with?

Still, if Bukowski found success in the 1950s, you can find it today.

Now let's explore some of the most popular myths about writing guest posts.

Myth: Your Editor Writes the Headline

The headline is the most important part of any article or blog post.

It's the first thing readers see, so it should persuade them to click on a link to your article.

When you're pitching an editor, include a strong headline following the style of the blog you're writing for. This practice is often enough to grab an editor's attention.

You can write a good headline by studying the five most popular blog posts on the site you're pitching.

Alternatively, examine the covers of popular magazines like *Cosmopolitan* or *Esquire* or other magazines in your niche.

Here's how:

1. Type "*Cosmo*" into Google Images search so you can see lots of magazine covers.

2. Pick several headlines from a magazine cover you like, for example "Get-fit secrets for a tight bod"

3. Adapt each headline around your topic, like "7 editing secrets for tight copy".

Myth: One Idea Will Woo Your Editor

If you include one idea, your chances of getting published depend solely on the merits of your single idea.

If you include two ideas, your editor has a dilemma.

If you include three ideas, your editor has options.

You don't need to go into great detail for each idea (and a time-strapped editor with a thousand emails to read won't thank you for a 1,000-word email). You do want to give your editor more than what they're expecting.

Myth: Take Your Time Writing the Post

If your guest post is accepted, either ask your editor for a deadline or submit a completed post within two weeks.

If you're worried, make life easier by writing a rough draft of your article before you pitch the editor in question.

This way you can rework your draft before submitting it.

But what if your post is rejected?

Don't worry.

You can still rework the idea for another website. If that fails, use the post on your blog.

Myth: Style Guidelines Are for Fools

Style or guest-posting guidelines differ from site to site, and woe be the writer who ignores them. Editors might ask writers to do things like:

- Hit a target word count
- Include an image for your post
- Link to other articles or influencers in your post
- Write a linking post on your website
- Email an editor rather than the site owner (more on this in a moment)

One site I pitched hid a password in the middle of their guest-posting guidelines and asked that serious writers (i.e., the ones who read the guidelines) include this password in their initial email.

On most sites, you can typically find the writing guidelines on the About page, the Contact page or another dedicated page on the site.

Myth: Relationships are Unimportant

I sometimes comment on site's popular posts before sending the editor a pitch.

This practice will help you develop a relationship with the site owner or editor.

I also share these posts multiple times using Twitter because it notifies the site owners I shared their posts.

This notification accelerates building a relationship with the site (who doesn't like their writing being shared?) and easier to get a response to my guest-post pitch.

I also recommend linking from posts on your site to the site in question.

This tactic is useful if you're targeting mid-level rather than top-level blogs. The former might not have that many links and will notice yours, whereas the latter will have thousands.

Myth: The Editor's Name Doesn't Matter

In his book *How to Win Friends and Influence People,* Dale Carnegie wrote that "Names are the sweetest and most important sound in any language."

Most larger websites employ a full-time editor who manages content on behalf of the site owner. Whatever you do, don't start your email by saying "Hi" and then moving into your pitch.

Your email pitch will sound cold and impersonal. The guest-posting guidelines of most sites often include the names of the editors. Use them.

Find out the editor's name.

If you're stuck, address the site owner by name.

Myth: Didn't Hear Back Immediately? Move On

The owners and editors of popular websites are busy people with even busier inboxes.

If they don't respond immediately to your initial guest-post pitch, don't take it personally. Instead, seven days after your pitch, send a follow-up email politely asking if they received your inquiry.

A week is long enough to avoid harassing the editor but not so long that they forget about you. In the majority of cases, the editor will respond to the follow-up submission.

Four of my five pitches received a response after I took this approach. If the editor still don't respond, try again in one week or take your idea to another website.

The web is a big place.

Myth: Your Job Is Over Upon Publication

Professional writers are always thinking about the next job. You should too.

When you write a guest post for a popular website, thank everybody who shares or comments on your post and respond to their comments.

If you have time, read the bios of those who share your posts on Twitter.

If these people have a relationship with a site you want to write for, contact them with a new guest post idea.

You will be fresh in their mind, and they will be receptive to your ideas for their site. A few days after your post is published, send the editor a short email thanking them for the opportunity.

This way you can keep the door open for future submissions. Even if you decide not to write for them again, this will leave a positive impression with the editor, which is the hallmark of a professional.

WIN NEW READERS FASTER

Friendship is a long-term game, and so is writing guest posts.

Yes, it takes some time to get started if you haven't written a guest post before.

However, after you've written several guest posts, the editors of larger and more popular websites will become more receptive to your ideas because you can point to a body of work.

Plus, you can use old posts to build your credibility with your audience.

Now go give your best work away for free.

If anyone asks, tell them Charles Bukowski sent you.

BUT I'M A WRITER, NOT A MARKETER!

Can I be blunt?

This is a cop-out, and it's one I spent years making.

I've sat in writing groups and listened to myself and my peers describe how marketing a book or a piece of writing is debasing. At the time, I agreed with the other members of these groups that marketing should be left to the marketers and writing to the writers.

We were wrong.

What's the point in writing if nobody reads your work?

In his book *All Marketers Are Liars*, the oracle of online marketing, Seth Godin, provides numerous examples of companies, brands and business people that tell authentic stories about their products.

He wrote, "When you find a story that works, live that story, make it true, authentic, and subject to scrutiny. All marketers are storytellers."

Did I mention Godin has published 17 books?

Don't feel bad or sleazy about these kinds of marketing activities.

Instead, you're telling stories about your work. These are stories you know well, but your future readers haven't heard them yet.

As a writer, your most important task for the day is to write. After all, you can't market your work if you haven't produced anything of value. However, your job doesn't end when you press submit or upload your new book to Amazon.

Research what your audience wants, build relationships with thought leaders who can help, and keep searching for ways to get in front of new readers. This is what the productive writer does.

He or she commits to connecting with readers and editors, and writing consistently.

EXERCISE LIKE YOUR CRAFT
DEPENDS ON IT

"Exerting yourself to the fullest within your individual limits: that's the essence of running, and a metaphor for life— and for me, for writing as well. I believe many runners would agree." – Haruki Murakami

Physical exercise is a worthy and important pursuit for the productive writer.

Haruki Murakami, the Japanese author of books like *Kafka on the Shore* and *After Dark*, says running and cycling help him become more creative.

When he's working on a novel, and after his work is complete for the day, Murakami swims for 1,500 metres or runs 10 kilometres. He maintains this routine almost every day.

He wrote, "For me, the main goal of exercising is to maintain, and improve, my physical condition in order to keep on writing novels."

Murakami knows what he's talking about.

According to Michael Mumford of the University of

Oklahoma, 30 minutes of aerobic exercise will help you become more creative.

Succeeding at intense physical activities takes focus, concentration and discipline, just like writing.

The creative process involves working hard on a single task at length, as do intense physical activities like swimming, cycling, football and so on.

When I'm stuck on a troublesome piece, I sometimes go for a run, a swim or a long walk. I'm not going to lie and say exercising is always easy and enjoyable. Still, this practice helps me cultivate discipline and focus.

There, in the pool or on the road, when I'm not thinking about writing at all, a solution arises, and I see a way through whatever problem I'm facing.

Thirty minutes of exercise a day isn't too much, especially if you're pursuing a craft that requires you to sit down for hours at a time. Exercising will give you more energy, a break and a new perspective on your work.

MEDITATE

Meditation, like exercise, can help you write too. Meditation and writing have a lot in common. They both involve sitting in one place and focusing on one task for extended periods of time.

Meditation is one of the best ways to spark creativity, improve focus and make you smarter. Dozens of high-profile studies demonstrate the links between meditation, creativity and focus.

For example, a 2012 scientific study by the Leiden University in the Netherlands found that "...meditation leads to better performance in a distributed-attention task and reinforces the view that meditation practice can have a lasting and generalizable impact on human cognition."

Sitting quietly on a cushion and focusing on your breath for just 15 minutes each day makes it easier to sit in front of a computer or the blank page and write for extended periods.

Meditation also serves as a necessary and welcome break from a computer screen or troublesome sentence. It won't solve your physical problems directly, but it will help you become more aware of when you need to take a break. And it can help you become more mindful of chronic pain.

The next time you're in a creative rut, put on a pair of runners or meditate on the problem.

VALUE YOUR HEALTH

Writing looks like an easy enough activity.

To the untrained observer, a writer sits on a comfortable chair, plucks words from a dictionary and spins an indulgent yarn.

For most writers, the craft of producing prose is anything but easy or magical.

Writing requires a certain degree of physical and mental endurance and focus. A writer has to sit in one spot for hours every day and sustain concentration for extended periods. And they have to do so alone without the distraction or encouragement of office colleagues or the material world.

A writer must have enough energy to sit and focus without becoming too distracted or tired to write. This kind of work is mentally exhausting. Physically, it can take its toll too.

Some days when I write for an extended period, my back aches, my eyes dry up, my hands cramp and my head spins. Then when I close my eyes, all I can see is floating black and white dots.

In 2014, I spent several weeks attending physiotherapy

sessions for sciatica. I experienced this pain up and down my legs because I was spending too much time sitting down.

You can overcome physical complaints like these by taking short but regular breaks from the screen or the blank page and exercising when you're not writing.

The physio prescribed several exercises. He also suggested that when practical I stand, for example while reading my work.

If you are in pain for another reason, say because of an illness, crafting a meaningful sentence is almost impossible.

How can you write while you head throbs?

If you are particularly stressed, angry or emotional, it's difficult to achieve the kind of focus necessary for extended periods of examination and good writing.

Contrary to popular belief, hangovers don't make for effective prose. We might find reading stories about a drunken night out entertaining, but it's almost always impossible to write under the influence or while hungover.

Even Hemingway and F. Scott Fitzgerald attempted to write soberly towards the end of their writing careers because they recognised being wildly intoxicated doesn't always make for wildly intoxicating prose or productive writing.

Fitzgerald famously said, "First you take a drink, then the drink takes a drink, then the drink takes you."

ACCEPT WRITING IS SOMETIMES PAINFUL

I'm talking about the deep introspective writing that real writers put themselves through.

Writing should almost never be physically painful.

If it hurts, get the opinion of an expert like I did.

My physical therapist provided me with an assessment and a series of exercises that worked.

I found paying a professional more productive than diagnosing myself by reading articles online and treating myself by watching YouTube videos.

Don't write while in pain if you can avoid it, and remember your health should come first. Otherwise, you won't accomplish much.

CONSERVE YOUR WILLPOWER

"The life of the professional writer – like that of any freelance, whether she be a plumber or a podiatrist – is predicated on willpower." – Will Self

"I just can't be bothered."

"I'm just too tired."

"I don't have the energy today."

Have you ever made these kinds of excuses when it's time to write?

If you have, don't beat yourself up. This form of procrastination is natural.

In a 2009 study, Roy Baumeister, a psychologist at Florida State University, carried out an experiment where he asked students to sit next to a plate of fresh-baked chocolate chip cookies.

He gave permission to some students to eat the cookies, and he told others to avoid eating any of them. Afterwards, Baumeister gave both groups difficult puzzles to solve.

The students who'd resisted eating the cookies found the

puzzles harder to complete, and they abandoned the task. Their mental resources were depleted.

But those students who ate the cookies worked on the puzzles longer. Baumeister found they were able to remain focused because they had more mental resources.

If you're working on a difficult writing project, your productivity will suffer if your willpower is running low. You're also more likely to experience a creative drought.

Have you ever experienced the following issues?

- You plan to write at the end of the day, only to come home exhausted and watch television instead.
- Your word counts are lower when you write while tired?
- You find it difficult to concentrate on writing projects after a stressful event or a busy morning.

If the answer is yes, a dearth of willpower affected your writing. The good news is it's easy to conserve your willpower, avoid a creative drought, have your cookies and eat them too.

HOW TO CONSERVE YOUR WILLPOWER

Anytime I avoid writing because I'm tired, bored or "not feeling it", I remind myself of the importance of self-discipline.

It's not sexy, but almost every writer I've read about sacrificed to pursue their work. They rose early or worked late into the night. And they wrote because they had to, not just when they felt the hand of inspiration.

Virginia Woolf wrote with a pencil and paper every morning until the early afternoon. She described writing and her ordinary moments. "I generally write with heat and ease till 12.30; and thus do my two pages. So it will be done, written over that is, in 3 weeks, I forecast from today."

So set yourself up for success the day before you get to work.

At the end of your day, prepare the next day's writing in advance. Decide what you're going to work on and for how long.

You could go as far as tidying your workspace, arranging your notes, and opening up the writing application on your computer. (See chapter 15).

The next morning when you wake and get to your desk, you won't have to make any decisions about your writing, and you won't have to waste time getting your tools or your project ready. All you have to do is sit down and do the work.

Another way to conserve your willpower is to decide on your most important tasks for the following day beforehand.

Productive people use this approach to accomplish more in the workplace. At the end of the day, spend five minutes writing down three to five tasks you want to accomplish the next day.

For example, you could decide to freewrite, edit and then market an article, in that order. You could decide to brainstorm, proofread and research a chapter of your new book. Or you could consider what you're going to do after you finish writing.

BALANCE COMPETING PRIORITIES

Determining your most important tasks each day forces you to review your commitments in advance.

These regular mini-reviews will give you a chance to check in with how your writing is progressing. You'll get into the habit of overcoming the hurdles preventing you from becoming a more productive writer.

The next day when you start work, progress through your most important tasks in order and first thing. The key is to finish these tasks before you check email, make phone calls, arrange meetings or meet with colleagues. Before you attend to things that pop up.

The majority of these other activities are items on someone else's To Do list. Yes, they might be important, but are they as important as your writing?

Remember, every time you say yes to someone else's priorities, you're saying no to your writing. Sometimes, being successful means being a little selfish.

You can also conserve and replenish your willpower by looking after yourself. You can do this by sleeping, eating healthily, exercising, meditating, doing the right thing at the right times, taking naps and listening to music.

Me?

I like writing first thing in the morning because it sets up the entire day. When I succeed, I feel like the entire day is golden because I put some words down onto the page, however ugly.

If a meeting runs over, if there's a last minute appointment or a crisis with a colleague, my day is still a good one.

PROTECT YOUR BEST SELF

Conserve your willpower for the moments when you really need it. For when it's time to write, to create, to live.

If you practice this strategy, you will find writing every day more natural, and you will gain the momentum you need to keep going – even when you want to stop.

When you're done, reward yourself with a cookie.

I won't tell anyone.

START A FIGHT

" A fter all, the ultimate goal of all research is not
objectivity, but truth." – Helene Deutsch

Ditch any notions you have about being an objective writer.

Take a stance.

Objectivity is a falsehood, and objective writing is a style of writing best left to serious journalists and scientists. Even then, the most seasoned journalists and scientific writers bring a natural level of subconscious bias to their writings.

They can write only through the frame of their upbringing, education and years of experience as a journalist or scientific writer. Everything else is second-hand information.

Yes, there are times when a writer should avoid inserting himself or herself directly into the piece they are working on, for example, a journalist writing about a natural disaster.

Yes, sometimes a writer should give information rather than opinion, for example, a scientist writing about a serious medical condition.

Mostly though, this kind of writing is boring and unnecessary. Almost nobody will read it.

When you write, take a stance. Have an opinion and pick a fight. Call out another writer or an expert in your field. Tell readers what you believe.

Argue for or against prevailing thinking. Explain your passion or what you've learnt. If the material you're working with is boring and grey, try and inject some colour.

You can take a stance by writing from the heart, or you can use calculated reasoning. Whatever your approach, nothing is less invigorating to read than an author planted undecidedly in the middle.

If you succeed, you will invoke a reaction in your readers. They might hate what you're saying or disagree with you entirely, but at least they're engaging with you.

Just remember that having a stance doesn't mean being vicious or nasty for the sake of it.

BE MODEST

Some readers will know less than you do; others will know more. Some will be interested in what you have to say, some will think you're wrong, and others just won't care.

Writers who try to impress readers with how much they know or how clever they are almost always fall flat on their faces. Those who hold back on the page for fear of embarrassment or because of foolish pride will produce a mediocre piece of work that will be forgotten.

If you want to avoid these pitfalls, reveal your weaknesses or faults. Let your readers know where you went wrong and how you're trying to improve (if at all).

It's OK to admit you don't know everything and that you made mistakes. These kinds of intimate details help readers relate to you.

Readers love brutal honesty because they've made mistakes too. Readers are not some homogenous group of people who judge your work as one. They're individuals who make mistakes, and they want to hear about yours.

If you're writing a more formal article, such as a step-by-step guide or tutorial, ask readers if they have any questions or suggestions at the end of your article. The best formal articles encourage discussion, debate or feedback.

I've tried to include as many practical writing tips as I could find and think of in this book, but I also accept that some more accomplished writers might have ideas I've yet to consider.

That's OK with me because through writing, I'm seeking to learn more about the craft of writing and share the learnings of my journey with you.

Don't you want to do the same?

PRACTICE HUMAN DECENCY

Somewhere, someone on the internet is wrong.

Is that person you?

Are you hiding behind your computer screen?

Have you ever ranted or told someone that their work is terrible and why they should never create again?

I'm being unfair – you strike me as an honest reader – but if you read the comments on popular YouTube videos, the reviews of books on Amazon or the comments on a popular forum post, you can find hundreds of examples of people who don't demonstrate common human decency.

Some commentators shout in CAPs. Meanwhile, others tell the creator that they've failed and should give up writing.

I've a confession to make.

Years ago, I was a little like that. I reviewed films for a

local newspaper. The newspaper didn't have a budget to send reviewers to the films, so I made up my reviews.

I wanted to make a name for myself, so I analysed and criticised the hard work of other creative professionals even though I hadn't watched their accomplishments or failures. It was an awful way to spend my time, and my reviews were terrible.

My editor was OK about it, but I lost my self-respect as a writer.

I learnt it's easier to attack someone's work for its obvious flaws than it is to take the time to leave your comfort zone, create something and put yourself out there by sharing your ugly bastard child with the world.

These days I write about something I like, use or am passionate about.

The act of writing is a gift that writers can use to bring light into dark places. For example, abrasive writers like Charles Bukowski were more concerned with their failings than the failings of others. He said, "If you're losing your soul and you know it, then you've still got a soul left to lose."

Today, I've a lot of respect for established reviewers and critics like American film critic Roger Ebert who died in 2013. The best critics value the creative arts, they're honest, and they engage with their readers.

If you must respond or critique other people's work, look for the higher ground. If the work you're reviewing is badly written, write a *constructive* critique.

Explain the negatives and the positives of someone's work. Or provide a personal context that helps the reader understand if the work in question is worth their time or money.

If work is ill-judged, explain why without humiliating the person on the other end. If this isn't possible, either don't write anything or think of a time when you wrote something that failed.

The productive writer – hell any writer – has failed at some point. All of us should appreciate how difficult creation is.

TELL A LIE

"Fiction is the lie that tells the truth, after all." – Neil Gaiman

Do you enjoy telling lies? Do you have a little something on the side? Are you cheating?

If want your writing to sparkle, you should. New writers sometimes feel paralysed because they are not an expert in their chosen topic or because they just can't think of a good or original idea.

After browsing Amazon or the shelves in a local bookstore, it feels like everything has been said, the best books are already published, and there are no good ideas left.

You've still got time. You can still capture a great idea. You've just got to fake it until you find one.

More experienced writers sometimes say they want to publish more of their work and more frequently, but they often feel hamstrung by deadlines and other professional commitments.

If you're having these kinds of creative problems, you've got to tell yourself a little white lie.

You've got to cheat.

You've got to have a little something on the side.

USE WHITE LIES

When I first started researching *The Savvy Writer's Guide to Productivity*, I lied to myself.

Despite the many great productivity books in publication, I told myself I could find something original to say. I told myself I could offer up fresh insight into the world of productivity.

The sad reality was that when I started this book, I didn't have any good ideas or fresh insights, but then a funny thing happened.

This white lie gave me enough momentum to start writing my book.

When I started writing my book, I began to apply what I discovered about productivity to the art of writing. Through doing this, I discovered a different perspective on both topics. Telling a lie to myself or faking it helped me finish writing my book.

There's a scientific merit to telling yourself white lies.

According to Dr. Paul Seager, a British psychology lecturer, telling a white lie is healthy. He said,

> To keep society running smoothly, we need to tell white lies. If your partner comes home with their latest piece of artwork and says, 'What do you think of this?', it shows they want support. Whether you like it or not, you're going to say it's nice.

Like the supportive partner, why not support your own

ideas and work?

Tell yourself you have something original to say even if you don't.

Later on, you'll find you do have something original to say after all. And if you're worried you've deluded yourself, you can always sense-check your ideas with the help of your editor, your writing group and anyone who reads early versions of your work.

FRESHEN UP YOUR WRITING

You can use a white lie to freshen up the way you write about an old topic.

For example, some social media experts claim Facebook is the perfect social media network for business people who want to talk to customers, or in our case writers who want to talk to their readers.

They cite Facebook's two billion users, ease of use and vast data points.

Let's assume these experts are wrong.

Let's tell a white lie to ourselves and say Facebook is the worst social media network for writers who want to talk to customers or readers.

Using this little lie, you write an article that calls on writers to abandon Facebook. Tell them to try Twitter, Instagram or Pinterest and explain how they can get started.

You can do this by writing about what happened when you took this approach. Or you could argue that writers should forget about social media and concentrate on building their email lists instead.

Then you could give your article a headline like:

"Forget Facebook: Your Email List is King"

Or

"What Facebook Isn't Telling You: 7 Shocking Secrets for Smart Writers"

I'm not suggesting you wilfully mislead your reader. Instead, the productive writer sometimes turns a fact on its head and attacks their project from a new and exciting angle.

They look for a way in that their peers haven't thought of. Don't believe me? Writers use this trick all the time.

How often have you clicked on articles with headlines like:

- Everything you know about X is wrong. Here's why
- The Shocking Truth about X
- The Great X Hoax
- 15 Things Your Favourite X Will Never Tell You
- What X Isn't Telling You about Y

These headline writers are using the power of a white lie to grab the attention of their readers. They are suggesting some deception because they know this will arouse curiosity within their readers. They know their readers will want to find out the truth.

HAVE A LITTLE SOMETHING ON THE SIDE

If you're bored with your current writing project, cheat. Walk out on what you're doing and start writing something that fires you up.

Having a writing project on the side can keep you motivated when your book, story or article is losing its lustre. This side project will give you a new chance to turn up in front of the blank page when you want to do anything but.

Many successful writers cheat. They use pseudonyms for their creative side projects.

Stephen King wrote several horror novels under the pen name Richard Bachman because he wanted to publish more than one novel per year. Between 1977 and 2007, King published seven novels using this pen name including *The Running Man* and *Thinner*.

King said he took on this side project because he didn't want to oversaturate his brand. He's not the only high-profile author to take on a side project or use a pen name.

In 2005, Irish literary author John Banville won the prestigious Man Booker prize for his novel *The Sea*. Then in 2006, Banville published the first of his popular series of crime novels under the pen name Benjamin Black.

Several years ago, I attended a talk by Banville in Kerry where he explained why he sometimes uses a pen name.

He told a room of over 100 people he wanted to write something that wasn't so serious and that he could write and publish faster. He wanted a side project he could turn to when he needed a break from writing literary fiction.

J.K. Rowling is another example of a writer with a side project. She has published three crime fiction novels under the pen name Robert Galbraith.

Rowling said,

> I had hoped to keep this secret a little longer, because being Robert Galbraith has been such a liberating experience. It has been wonderful to publish without hype or expectation, and pure pleasure to get feedback under a different name.

Having a side project gives writers opportunities to explore new writing styles and conventions that they typically wouldn't face othewise.

This form of deliberate writing practice will help you become a better writer. It will help you avoid the exhaustion and burnout that comes with focusing solely on a single niche or topic.

TAKE ON SIDE PROJECTS

If your day job involves writing reports, articles or copy for a website, you could write fiction in your free time.

If you spend most of your time writing blog posts, consider expanding one of these posts into a book or a personal essay. And if you've just written a novel, try your hand at a short story in a different genre.

Before you cheat, remember finishing one writing project is usually more productive than attempting two at once.

Now if you're confident you have the time and motivation to write and finish two projects, have a little something on the side.

I won't tell anyone if you won't.

SEEK OUT QUIET SPACES

"Weakness of attitude becomes weakness of character." – Albert Einstein

Are you able to work like Albert Einstein?

He researched and wrote some of his groundbreaking scientific papers while at home, surrounded by his two small children. Einstein could write and think anywhere.

"Even the loudest baby-crying didn't seem to disturb Father," said Hans Albert about his father. "He could go on with his work completely impervious to noise."

Most of us don't have Albert Einstein's genius, talent or focus.

Carving out a quiet space in your house or workplace will help you write and think. Going to this place at the same time every day simplifies sitting in front of the blank page and writing when you want to do anything but.

I have two small children, and it's difficult to write when they are nearby. Instead, I get up early in the morning to write before they rise. I go to a small room near the front of the house and write until they get up.

This quiet time enables me to focus for longer and write more frequently than my failed attempts to write in the evenings when my house is noisier and busier.

Even if you don't have children, eliminate as many distractions as you can from your writing room or office.

This means no televisions, game consoles, mobile devices and, in certain cases, internet connections. A window, heating and air conditioning are nice, but they're not necessary. A good desk, pens, paper and an idea are all you need.

In *On Writing* Stephen King says about having a quiet room in which to work:

> Like your bedroom, your writing room should be private, a place where you go to dream.
>
> Your schedule — in at about the same time every day, out when your thousand words are on paper or disk — exists in order to habituate yourself, to make yourself ready to dream just as you make yourself ready to sleep by going to bed at roughly the same time each night and following the same ritual as you go.

GO SOMEWHERE NEW TO WRITE

I'm contradicting myself, but a productive writer must be able to have two competing ideas in his or her head.

Nobody said our craft is easy.

Writing in a new environment will break your mind free from the shackles of comfortable thinking.

Going to a new location to write can get you out of a creative rut and help you overcome hurdles on the blank page. Sometimes, a new angle of attack will help you finish what you started.

At the end of the first *Star Wars* movie, Luke Skywalker flies into the trench of the Death Star.

At first, Luke follows the same approach as every other fighter pilot and for a few terrible moments it looks like he will be killed by Darth Vadar's minions.

Then Obi-Wan Kenobi tells Luke to "use the Force". So, Luke turns off all his instruments and attacks the Death Star. Using this new approach, Luke succeeds at something no pilot had done before: he destroys the Death Star.

This *Star Wars* example represents storytelling at its finest, and it shows taking a different angle of attack can help you overcome a problem.

In case you're not a Star Wars fan, I've dug up some scientific proof that supports writing in a new environment and coming at your project from an oblique angle.

A 2012 study in the *Journal of Consumer Research* found ambient or background noise positively affects creativity and increases the chances of innovative thinking. The authors Ravi Mehta, Rui Zhu and Amar Cheema wrote:

> Results from five experiments demonstrate that a moderate (70 dB) versus low (50 dB) level of ambient noise enhances performance on creative tasks and increases the buying likelihood of innovative products.

The key takeaway from this report is to find somewhere with a comfortable but not distracting level of background noise. So while a coffee shop might be appropriate, a playground full of children or a noisy bar won't help.

MANAGE YOUR ENVIRONMENT

If you work in an office, you could write at another desk or outside the office. I once worked in an office that had small rooms or booths that could fit only one person at a time.

These booths were designed for making private phones calls away from the noise of the office, but I used them to write website copy and blog posts for the company.

I accomplished more there because I was less likely to be interrupted by the phone, email or a noisy colleague.

Later, when I needed feedback about my copy, I went back to my desk and asked my colleagues for advice.

If your computer is the problem, leave it behind. Take a notepad and pen and go outside. The stimulation of a new environment combined with the openness of pen and paper might help you find your next sentence.

Pen and paper open the mind to new ideas in a way that the screen can't.

You could go to your local library and combine a morning's writing with an afternoon's research.

Several years ago I had to write a 20,000-word thesis. I found it easier to write my thesis in the college library even though I had a perfectly good office at home.

This wasn't just because the library had everything I needed for my research; after all, I could have always rented the books I needed and took them home with me.

It felt liberating to escape from where I normally worked, and I found finishing my work less stressful.

Sometimes writers need a quiet place and a routine to get more done, and sometimes they need to attack their project from a new angle. Or you could just use the Force.

Whatever works.

WRITE IN SHORT BURSTS

"I had to make sure I kept an eye on the real world." – Roddy Doyle

Short writing sessions are the best kind.

If you're struggling to develop a productive and regular writing habit, try writing every day for 15 or 30 minutes.

This is easier to achieve than sitting in front of the blank page for several hours every other Sunday. This goal is achievable as almost every aspiring writer has 15-30 minutes in their day of which they can use more wisely.

If writing isn't your full-time job, short writing sessions are perfect for busy days. You could write between meetings, on the bus or train, before you leave for work or late in the evening.

If you want to write in the evenings, you could skip a television programme, avoid the news or reduce the amount of time you spend on social media.

To get more from your next short writing session try:

- Creating a list of topics to include in your article
- Jotting down key words and ideas instead of full sentences
- Forgetting about perfect grammar, spelling or formatting
- Using pen and paper instead of a computer
- Setting yourself a challenge to produce as many words as possible within five, 10, 20 or 30 minutes
- Focusing on a single angle, section or paragraph
- Writing with the intention that you will fix or flesh out your ideas tomorrow

Short bursts of writing are like small wins. They accumulate over time until one day you look at your work and realise you've written 10,000 words.

LEARN FROM RODDY DOYLE

Irish author Roddy Doyle is famous for writing succinct and punchy sentences.

I attended a workshop about writing that he facilitated several years ago in Dublin. Roddy explained that he wrote his earlier books during pockets of free time in the evenings.

He also said the sentences in earlier books like *The Commitments* and *The Snapper* are short because he wrote them while raising small children.

Roddy just didn't have time for lengthy, three-hour writing sessions, and if he didn't write in short bursts he wouldn't have written at all.

Doyle has even criticised other, more wordy books for being too long and unapproachable. In New York in 2014, he said, "*Ulysses* could have done with a good editor. You know people are always putting *Ulysses* in the top 10 books ever written but I doubt that any of those people were really moved by it."

I have two small children, and I can empathise with writers who must work within short blocks of time. Sometimes, the prospect of several hours' work feels more intimidating than the job of sitting down for just 30 minutes to write.

I also like short writing sessions because I feel like I've accomplished something for the day, and that can be enough to build the momentum needed to continue a troublesome writing project.

T.S. Eliot is another noted writer who wrote around the demands of his day. He worked at Lloyds Bank in London for much of his adult life, and he wrote book reviews and poetry in his free time.

Eliot kept his job in the bank after he became an accomplished poet, as his job provided him with a stabilising routine that he valued as a writer.

More recently, Doyle is quoted as saying that he now spends up to nine hours a day writing. Still, his and Elliot's experiences show a writer can finish what they started, even if they have commitments.

All you need is determination.

ESTABLISH A DAILY WRITING PRACTICE

This time things were supposed to different.

Late last night, you promised yourself you'd write today. Then you woke half an hour late for work. You got stuck in traffic and spent the day dealing with an angry customer/client/boss.

Later that evening at home, your kids needed help with their homework, and you had chores to do around the house.

When things were finally quiet, you didn't have the desire

or the energy to sit down and do your most important work. Or maybe you forgot about your promise altogether.

To write every day is a simple ambition, and it's one many new writers struggle to achieve.

If you're having trouble, don't give up.

I don't doubt your commitment or your talent; the only reason you don't write every day is because you haven't cultivated a daily writing practice.

In his book *The Power of Habit,* author and journalist Charles Duhigg provides a simple but effective framework for creating habits. He said that, "Habits are a three-step loop — the cue, the routine, and the reward."

SET UP YOUR CUES FOR WRITING

A habitual cue is something you see or do before you start writing. If you want to develop a writing practice, consider these cues.

Location: Know in advance where you're going to write. This could be your office, a quiet room in your house or a coffee shop.

Time: Commit to writing at the same time every morning or evening. Don't make any plans that break this commitment

Emotional state: If you're stressed after a difficult day in the office, you'll find it harder to write. Figure out when you're calm and use this time for your best work.

Other people: Writing is mostly a solitary activity, but the support or critique of other writers is useful too. You could join a local writing group to hold yourself to account.

Immediately preceding action: Whatever you do before you write should encourage your writing practice. If you're exhausted from spending the night at a party, you're not going to have much luck filling a blank page.

If you want to write every day, kill the cues for other habits that have nothing to do with your writing practice.

Do WHATEVER IT TAKES to keep your promise to protect your writing time and complete your most important work. (See chapter 10).

STICK TO YOUR WRITING ROUTINE

Routines are powerful because we don't have to think about them. If you spend your day wondering how and where you're going to write, these questions will drain your mental willpower and make you more likely to say, "I'll do it tomorrow."

A good writing routine will help you overcome procrastination, become more productive and shape your creative life.

If you want to spend less time thinking about your routine:

Gather what you need in advance. If you spend precious writing time searching for a laptop charger, your notes or for a file on your computer, you're already behind.

Use the same tools each time. I use Scrivener for almost all of my writing projects; whatever you use, the tool should never get in the way your writing.

Make a choice to trigger your cue. If you want to write in the morning, set your alarm clock for an hour earlier. If you want to write at night, turn off your phone and television and disconnect from the grid.

When you're starting out, it helps to decide in advance what you're going to write about.

Are you writing a blog post, short story or a chapter for your novel? What topic are you going to address today?

This decision will help you avoid the horrible moment when you sit down in front of the blank page and wonder, "What now?"

PICK YOUR REWARD FOR WRITING

Writing is tough and even more so when you're starting out.

Go easier on yourself.

If you succeed in writing for 20 minutes, reward yourself with a treat like a cookie.

If you can chain three or four 20-minute sessions together, go for a walk, sleep or watch a favourite television programme. If you succeed in finishing an important writing project, buy something for yourself.

When I completed my thesis, I bought an expensive a entertainment system that I otherwise couldn't have justified. This reward system will trick your brain into associating pleasant activities with your writing practice.

Obviously it's not practical to eat a cookie (or to spend several hundred dollars) for every page. However, as you become more confident, you can extend the length and quality of your writing practice sessions and gradually remove these rewards.

If you succeed in cultivating a habit of writing every day, filling the blank page with your words and making small but determined progress towards a personal or professional goal will become a reward in itself.

MAKE A PLAN AND STICK TO IT

Once you've figured out your cue, routine and reward for writing, have a plan for putting this into action. Duhigg suggests people can make a plan for habit change by keeping a diary.

Here's an entry in my writing diary:

Where am I? At home
What time is it? 07.00

What's your emotional state? Tired but calm
Who else is around? Wife and two children (asleep)
What action preceded the urge to write? My alarm clock went off.

I also sometimes record what I wrote about during writing practice and what I'd like to focus on next. I don't write entries like this all the time, but they help me when I'm stuck.

Seeking out this kind of self-knowledge will help you identify your cue, routine and reward for writing.

WRITE EVERY DAY

Creating a habit of daily writing practice isn't as difficult as it first seems. It takes determination and self-knowledge, and these are all traits every writer should cultivate.

Commit to this craft, and you will naturally become more determined as you progress. Learn to enjoy seeing your work improve, and you will come to value writing practice.

Take Duhigg's tips for cultivating a habit, and you will gain the self-knowledge you need to write every day.

If you're about to apply this plan, I envy you.

One day, you'll stop typing, realise you've written 3,000 words in one session, and you'll wonder, "How the hell did I get here?"

Now, go write something.

TRACK YOUR PROGRESS

"After a few days you'll have a chain. Just keep at it and the chain will grow longer every day. You'll like seeing that chain, especially when you get a few weeks under your belt. Your only job next is to not break the chain." – Jerry Seinfeld

How many words did you write today? Did you accomplish more than yesterday? And while I'm asking questions, did you write more this week or last week?

Almost every personal productivity strategy involves tracking your progress on some level because what gets tracked gets managed and what gets managed gets done.

Let me explain.

Professional athletes track themselves or use self-quantification techniques to record their diet, how much they lifted, how far they ran and how many lengths they swam and so on.

They use this information to train harder and smarter

and to perform better in events. Writers can use this approach to become more productive too.

You can track your time (which I'll cover in the next chapter) or your output.

KNOW THY WORD COUNT

Writers talk in terms of word counts rather than pages. They care less about page counts because the number of pages a piece takes depends on how the fonts, spacing and images are set and laid out. A page count is fluid, whereas a word count is less so.

I've met writers who use daily word counts for personal competitions; they make a point of breaking their personal bests just like the runner in search of a faster time.

I respect word counts because they can break a writer out of a creative funk and help you find something worthwhile to say. Knowing their average daily word counts can help writers achieve more.

For example, if your word count rises when you write in the morning and drops when you write at night, use this new information to cultivate an early morning writing habit.

Obsessing about word counts comes with a caveat. They are no indication of quality, as a particular type of writing demonstrates.

FLASH FICTION

Flash fiction is a special form of fiction writing for those who want to tell a story using as few words as possible. One of the most famous flash fiction stories (which might have been attributed to Hemingway) is just six words long.

For sale: baby shoes, never worn.

Behold the power of brevity.

This is why I also track how long I spend writing each week. While working on this book, I set myself the goal of writing 10,000 words a week or 10 hours a week.

I used a spreadsheet to do this.

Each Friday, I totalled up how long I spent writing and how many words I produced. This way, I could see how my book was progressing in terms of a word count and hours spent writing.

This self-quantification helped me during the editing process too because although I cared less about reaching a specific word count, I still needed a goal to write towards.

USE SMALL DAILY WINS

Getting the most from small daily wins means working on something a little every day and accomplishing your goals over time rather than trying to finish everything at the last minute.

Consider putting a euro or a dollar in a jar every day to save; it'll take you some time, but you'll get there in the end.

Now if you want to harness the power of small daily wins, I recommend a simple trick invented by a famous (and rich) comedian.

DON'T BREAK THE CHAIN

Comedian Jerry Seinfeld invented this popular productivity trick to motivate himself to write one new joke every day. It's built on the principle of increasing your creative output through small, daily wins.

I've used "Don't Break the Chain" to write feature articles, news stories, a thesis, academic papers, blog posts and this book.

If you procrastinate about sitting down in the front of the blank page regularly, this technique can help you get your ass into the chair. Here's how you do it:

1. Get a large calendar and pin it on the wall next to where you write.
2. Write for 5, 10, 20 or 30 minutes.
3. Using a felt pen, mark an X on your wall calendar through today's date.
4. As the week progresses, write each day and build up a series or a chain of Xs.
5. Now you have one job: Don't Break the Chain.

Don't Break the Chain makes you feel guilty about ruining a productive writing streak.

After all, nobody wants to a see a chain of Xs for every day spent writing, only to break this row because of procrastination.

I'm speaking from personal experience when I say it's encouraging and reassuring to see the black Xs line up one after the other as a project processes. Each little X feels like a small victory in the war against procrastination.

This strategy is useful at the beginning of larger, more difficult writing projects. It gets you into the habit of turning up each day and slowly progressing your project.

It will help you accept that, even if today's writing session doesn't go well, there is always tomorrow's session and the one after that. What's more important is that you turn up and put the work in.

There's just one problem with Seinfeld's technique. It's an unforgiving method because there's no allowances for going on holidays, falling sick or other personal commitments.

Hey, maybe Seinfeld doesn't get sick or take holidays?

Don't Break The Chain

A sample Don't Break the Chain chart

EMPOWER YOURSELF

The productive writer knows how much she can accomplish on the blank page each day.

She uses the power of small daily wins to write consistently rather than leaving everything till the last minute. Sometimes, she uses little tricks to write more frequently, like *Don't Break the Chain*.

She knows it's better to turn up and do the work than to do nothing altogether.

MANAGE YOUR TIME

"It's really clear that the most precious resource we all have is time." – Steve Jobs

Do you know how to manage your time?

The productive writer does. He understands how long his writing projects will take, he takes charge of his other commitments so they don't impact his work, and he gets the most out of the time he has for writing each day.

This is something I learnt the hard way.

For several years, I worked as a technology freelance journalist, and I made money through writing commissions for magazines in Ireland.

Although some commissions paid by the hour, editors still expected me to complete them by a deadline. For others, I was paid only for getting the job done.

This kind of freelance work meant I earned less for my time if I spent twenty hours on a commission that should have taken only ten hours. I learned the hard way that earning a living from writing means finishing freelance projects on time.

USE YOUR CALENDAR

Some professional writers book periods for writing each morning and/or evening in their calendars.

They avoid making personal or professional commitments during these times because they consider themselves "committed" to their writing. They treat their craft like a job with professional obligations that must be honoured.

The calendar is the productive freelancer's best friend. It should be yours too. Get deadlines and appointments out of your head and into Google calendar, Outlook or some other tool you trust.

Then check your calendar each morning or evening. At the end of every working week, spend 20 minutes reviewing the entries in your calendar too.

Check what's coming up for the next seven days and how you spent your time over the previous seven days. While reviewing your calendar, ask questions like:

- What took up the most of my time last week?
- Are these activities likely to reoccur?
- What resources do I need to complete these activities faster?
- What do I need to prioritise next week?
- Am I likely to meet or miss my imminent deadlines?
- What's my most important task next week?

MANAGE AN EDITORIAL CALENDAR

Editorial calendars are another great way of managing your time, particularly if you work with other writers or if you are a blogger.

The editors of professional media organisations use editorial calendars to plan writing projects in advance and to allow teams to juggle projects.

You can use an editorial calendar to map articles, stories, blog posts or chapters that you'd like to write over the next few months. This will help you gauge if you're progressing towards your writing goals.

You can keep an editorial calendar in a notebook, spreadsheet, file on your computer or on a digital calendar. Whatever your tool of choice, an editorial calendar should identify some or all of the below issues:

- The topic
- The deadline
- The resources required
- The state of the project i.e., first draft, second draft, etc.
- The publication date
- The priority of the writing project
- The media outlet or platform e.g., blog post, newsletter, social media

MAKE FRIENDS WITH DEADLINES

Deadlines are the productive writer's best friend; don't let anyone tell you otherwise.

Several years ago, I attended a workshop by Irish short story writer Claire Keegan. She explained that when she was starting off as a fiction writer, she used submission deadlines for short story competitions as something to work towards.

"Deadlines are not to be feared," she said. "They add a sense of urgency to our work."

Claire's point struck a chord with me, perhaps because I wasn't long out of college. Some writers (or students) leave writing projects till the last minute.

When the deadline looms, they stay up late the night before smoking, drinking coffee and working hard on their projects. If you went to college, you're probably familiar with this last-minute approach.

Professional writers like Keegan use deadlines to write more often. Amateur writers skip right past deadlines and tell editors their articles or stories will be ready when they're finished.

If you're good, you can get away with telling your editor to wait. For the rest of us mere mortals, staying up late the night before a deadline might accomplish the task, but it's not a great way to work or write.

In the past, I missed deadlines because I was overworked, sick, unfocused and disorganised.

My editors made allowances when I was overworked, understood when I sick, chastised me when I was unfocused and gave their next commission to someone else when I was disorganised.

If you're going to write for someone else, accept deadlines as part of your life. Respect them. Put them in your calendar and be honest about your ability to hit them.

Deadlines give productive writers a goal or endpoint to write towards. They force us to make decisions and *commit*. A looming deadline can cause stress and anxiety, but this kind of tension is natural when it comes to hard work.

MEET YOUR WRITING DEADLINES

If you're having trouble meeting deadlines try the following tactics:

- Keep a list of your projects, assign a deadline to each project and review this list each week
- Break projects into mini-projects with supporting deadlines
- Focus on the first or next action you need to take to advance a project
- Make more time for projects that are causing stress
- Diary your deadlines in a trusted system
- Communicate your deadlines to colleagues
- Abandon projects that won't help you achieve your goals in favour of higher-value projects
- Examine why you missed deadlines in the past
- Use existing deadlines as a reason for saying no to new projects

These days, I set myself artificial or soft deadlines for my writing projects. This helps me focus on what I'm writing, and it also gives me time to review and polish my work before publishing it.

Even if this approach doesn't work for you, ask yourself why you missed deadlines in the past and how you're going to solve this problem.

As a productive professional writer, you must finish your writing projects on time.

Almost every writer will tell you that finishing one project before a deadline makes it easier to finish the next one on time.

CONTROL SOCIAL MEDIA

To some people this is sacrilege, but unless social media is your business, it's a side attraction.

You can use social media to promote your work, engage with readers and research your market. However, if you're doing this at the expense of writing and finishing what you are working on, then you are wasting valuable time.

Spend your time writing, and afterwards approach social media as a way of amplifying existing content and a free market research tool.

GET PAID

Freelance journalists learn how to write fast. They need to eat, sleep and work on their next commission.

When I received my first 3,000-word commission from a national newspaper, I spent an entire week working on it. I carried out multiple long interviews and spent hours researching the topic online and offline.

I probably shouldn't be telling you this, but much of my research and interviews were unnecessary. I had to cut this extra work from the piece, and I still struggled to finish the article on time.

Later that month I was paid for the article itself and not how long I spent on it, which meant I'd put in a lot of unnecessary extra work.

I wasn't always paid per commission when I worked as a journalist. Several editors paid me in terms of hours spent on a writing project and not for how many words I wrote. These editors provided me with guidelines about how long a commission should take. In other words, I couldn't bill an editor for 20 hours of work for a 300-word article.

Getting paid by the hour meant I had to complete writing

projects within a set time period. If I spent too long on a commission, I was effectively paid less per hour.

If I completed a project too quickly, it was either of poor quality (in which case my editor was quick to let me know) or I was paid less money.

So I started tracking how long I spent on each commission using a timer on my computer and a spreadsheet. This information simplified invoicing clients too.

It also helped me figure out which kinds of commissions were easy to complete, which were more difficult and how I could become a more productive writer. I also used this information to set prices for other clients and to decide which commissions to accept and reject.

Figuring out how long to spend on a commission is a difficult balancing act. Give yourself some breathing room before you tell your editor how long you need. If you think a commission will take six hours to complete, tell your editor it will take seven or eight hours.

This way, if there's an unforeseen circumstance, such as an interviewee cancelling at last minute, you will have extra time to complete your project. And if the commission takes only six hours, you can please your editor by under-promising and over-delivering.

Tracking your writing might seem tedious at first, but it will help you figure out which projects are taking longer than others, how you can complete these projects quicker and if you should accept or reject certain projects in the future.

This process will also save you time submitting invoices at the end of the month, and it will give you confidence to negotiate a better rate from an editor or client.

SPEND YOUR REWARD

If you're having trouble managing how you spend your time on projects, review your calendar and commitments, do your most important work when you're productive, and track what's working and what's causing you problems.

Succeed, and you will become a productive writer who has time to find new commissions or take a break.

Fail to manage your time effectively and your work will either spill into your personal life or dry up.

Remember, the productive writer who manages her time effectively also gives herself permission to take a break. The productive writer knows when she needs to eat, sleep and recharge.

Most importantly, she knows when to stop.

FOCUS ON YOUR WORK

"It does not matter how slowly you go as long as you do not stop." – Confucius

Flow is a productive mental state whereby you are entirely focused on the task at hand. If you've ever exercised intensively or lost yourself to a piece of music, you've experienced flow.

If you've ever started writing and lost track of the passage of time, you've experienced flow. It's a mental state you must seek if you want to become a more productive and accomplished writer.

An ability to focus on the task at hand is an important skill to cultivate.

The problem is technology wants us to do anything but. Phones, emails, notifications, feeds, applications and updates all pull on our attention throughout the day.

According to a report by Carnegie Mellon University published in the *New York Times*, a typical office worker is interrupted every 11 minutes. The researchers found it can take 21 minutes to refocus on a task, once interrupted.

This finding suggests it's almost impossible for the average office worker to experience flow because of these day-to-day interruptions.

Writing is not meant to be multi-tasked with answering email, checking social media and attending to the 1,001 other demands.

If you approach your craft with a start-stop-start mindset, you will never achieve the kind of flow writers need to reach the end.

The belief that multi-tasking helps people get more done faster is another pernicious myth. It taxes your brain and complicates finishing your writing project.

MIT neuroscientist Earl Miller told NPR in 2008, "Switching from task to task, you think that you're actually paying attention to everything around you at the same time. But you're not."

A true writer can't pay attention to everything around them at the same time.

How can you write one true sentence when you're checking your friend's holiday photos on Facebook?

How can you craft a perfect call-to-action for your copy when you're on the phone with a colleague?

How can you massage a paragraph into something readable when you're clicking from one blog post or website to another searching for something, *anything* that backs up your argument?

Commit yourself entirely to writing, and then when you're finished for the day, commit to whatever else is important.

HOW TO MAINTAIN FOCUS AND FLOW

Did you ever sit down to write and almost immediately think of something you forgot to look up?

When was the last time you put down your writing so you could research a new angle for your work?

Do you sometimes stop typing and pick up a book to check a fact or a quote?

I get it.

Research forms the backbone of many successful writing projects.

Academic writers, journalists, bloggers and writers interview experts, read books, search for topics online and go through the archives of their libraries.

Many writers enjoy research because they get to spend time talking to people and learning about topics in their area of interest. They enjoy it because writers like reading and finding out new things.

Research is an altogether different skill from writing. It involves moving from one question to the next, following a thread or searching for a specific piece of information.

Writing, on the other hand, means working deliberately on one sentence or idea for an extended period without giving up.

These two activities are almost impossible to undertake simultaneously. You can't jump from one topic to the next and concentrate entirely on a sentence or an idea.

Next time you're working and you want to check an important fact or how a word is spelt, DON'T STOP WRITING.

If you do, you will break your flow of concentration and possibly disappear down a rabbit hole of meaningless Google searches and needless research.

Instead, **annotate** the section of the document you are

writing with an asterisk, an X or with your writing programme's annotation tool. When you've hit your target word count for the day, address these annotations.

Commit yourself entirely to writing and entirely to research, just not at the same time. When I work this way, I'm always amazed by how a seemingly important question didn't need to be answered after all.

Similarly, **keeping a notepad and pen at your desk** will help you concentrate on what you're writing.

Use this notepad to record ideas or thoughts that come to mind. Record things you want to look up on the internet, people you want to call and food you have to buy. If a colleague drops by your desk with a request, record their request and then keep writing.

Unless the task or request is urgent, like a hungry child or an iron still plugged in, don't get up and do it. Later, when you're finished writing, you can spend time attending to the tasks on your notepad.

The purpose of annotating your work and using a notepad is to help you maintain a sense of flow.

This way, you can concentrate on your work. Later, you can concentrate on whatever else you want to do.

TIPS FOR FOCUSING ON YOUR WRITING

- Don a pair of noise-cancelling headphones and listen to white noise on repeat (look for albums of rainfall by Joe Baker on Spotify).
- Use a timer and work on one thing until the buzzer sounds.
- Disconnect from the internet while you write.
- Remove all distractions from where you write e.g. a television, games on your computer etc.

- Set aside time after your writing for doing something unproductive guilt-free like checking your Facebook feed.
- Leave your phone in a different room on silent.

MAINTAIN FOCUS

The productive writer knows it's difficult to get into the mindset needed to finish a project. He knows multitasking is a dangerous myth that stands in the way of his word count or writing milestone.

He knows his research, editing, writing, reading and so on are all different activities, and he doesn't try to do them all at once. Instead, he brings a single-minded focus to the blank page, and this is how he finishes writing what he started.

LET YOUR WRITING FERMENT

"The truth will set you free. But not until it is finished with you." – David Foster Wallace

Do you enjoy the taste of wine?

The best-tasting vintages are left to ferment for weeks, months or years in a cool, dark place before being decanted into bottles.

Winemakers and drinkers know the product becomes better with age. Writing is a little like making fine wine.

You must gather ingredients, equipment and materials. Both professions demand artistry, hard-work and craft.

Inevitably, it pays to wait for something good.

When you've worked on a difficult writing project at length, it's hard to know what to remove and what to keep.

When you're writing with flavour, should you cut a chapter or expand a key point? Should you insert more research or write a personal story?

These creative problems can become so exhausting you just want your writing project to end.

These kinds of creative problems are also natural. The more you write, the more comfortable you'll become with such challenges.

DON'T PRESS PUBLISH IMMEDIATELY

Don't publish a piece of writing immediately after you've reached the end.

It'll be too raw and bitter for public consumption. Every writer needs a dark place for their work to ferment.

Leave your early drafts in a drawer and rest, write something else, and forget about what's fermenting. Later, take this writing out into daylight and taste it. Approach it with an editing pen and a set of fresh eyes.

Thanks to this time away from your work, you will discover flaws and gaps you overlooked. You'll be able to address your problems with renewed vigour. You'll be able to write with flavour.

Unlike before, this rewrite will feel more natural. The solutions you searched for last time round will be within your reach.

When you finally publish your writing, your readers will enjoy the taste more, because you gave the flavour time to develop.

DECIDE HOW LONG TO WAIT

The time a piece of writing belongs in a drawer depends on how long it is, who it's for and your other professional commitments.

I let blog posts rest a day or two before publishing them. It's easier and faster to edit or change a blog post. If it's a longer article, I wait a week or more before sending it to an editor.

This is because I've professional relationships with editors who expect a certain standard of work.

I've also put my short stories and book chapters in a drawer for several months until I've almost forgotten what they're about.

This gives me time to cast a fresh eye over my work, remove clichés (there's one), ttypos (there's another) and fix other structural problems.

These different fermentation periods give me the distance I need to improve my writing.

I embrace this time away, because when I finally take my writing from the drawer, I'm fresh enough to expand, clarify or condense my points and sentences. I have the energy to back up my arguments with additional research.

Thanks to the drawer, I can face that much needed, and often dreaded rewrite with a thirst to fix what's broken. The drawer is a good place to let your writing ferment, but as a professional writer, you won't always be able to rely on this luxury.

LEARN FROM PROFESSIONAL WRITERS

Professional writers can't always put a piece of writing into a drawer and let it sit for weeks at a time. They have to work to deadlines imposed by editors, contracts, publications and even their readers. This is why professional writers don't work alone.

They invariably have the support of editors, who can catch these errors and mistakes. Supportive editors will show the writer how to avoid these kinds of errors in future.

Becoming a professional writer means enlisting an editor who serves as your ally in the war against perfectionism.

BEHOLD THE MYTH OF PERFECTIONISM

Writing with flavour doesn't mean waiting for the day when it's finally perfect. Even wine becomes undrinkable if it's left to ferment too long.

Remember, the perfect creative work doesn't exist.

A vast chasm exists between your ideas and how your words gather on the page. This chasm makes many writers and creative people feel squeamish. The philosopher, Nietzsche said, "And if thou gaze long into an abyss, the abyss will also gaze into thee."

When I see my words arranged on the page, I remember everything has already been said and in more ways than I can ever imagine.

The gaze of all those more talented and creative writers from times past gazes back at me. And I want to jump.

So I turn away.

And I press publish.

BEWARE OF PERFECTIONISM

If you insist on endlessly polishing and rewriting your work, you will delay your writing projects indefinitely.

This procrastination will frustrate colleagues, clients and readers (yes, your readers!), who are waiting for you to finish your work.

I hate to break it to you, but perfectionism is an excuse for putting off publishing your work. These kinds of excuses are indulgent.

Eventually, they turn the productive writer into a miserable, procrastinating failure.

The good news is, you can overcome perfectionism today.

CONQUER YOUR DEMONS

In a 1996 interview with radio station WYNC, American essayist and author David Foster Wallace explained the dangers of perfectionism:

> You know, the whole thing about perfectionism. The perfectionism is very dangerous, because of course if your fidelity to perfectionism is too high, you never do anything.
>
> Because doing anything results in– It's actually kind of tragic because it means you sacrifice how gorgeous and perfect it is in your head for what it really is.

I try to remember Wallace's advice when I approach the end of a writing project. I set publication dates for my writing, do my best to stick to them and occasionally have a little fun with the written word.

All I can do is keep practicing, falling forwards and using these painful writing lessons to improve my work.

If you're struggling to expose the myth of perfectionism in your writing, don't endlessly work and rework your writing alone.

So, whom can you ask for help?

An editor, trusted friend, member of your writing group or an honest family member all can help. The only caveat is this person must be able to offer you candid feedback you will act on.

Don't wait years to publish your writing.

Accept doubt as part of the process and understand you must share your writing with the world. Put it in the drawer and let your writing develop. Then take it out and release your work into the world.

Let them love it or hate it and all its ugly imperfections.

ASK FOR HELP

"We are all here on earth to help others; what on earth the others are here for I don't know." – W.H. Auden

There's no shame in it.

Writing might be a solitary craft, but if you're going to succeed with your writing, help is key.

You could look for a more experienced writer to act as your mentor or join a local writing critique group.

You might need to hire a designer to create a cover for your ebook or images for your website. Or you could hire someone to market and publicise your work or your business.

You can learn how to do all of these things yourself, but consider where your time is better spent: learning a skill secondary to your craft or writing?

Don't be all things when one is enough. The secret to becoming a more productive writer is to leverage your strengths and offset your weaknesses.

- Can you find an assistant for your research?
- Can an editor help you organise your work?
- Should you a hire a designer to create your book cover so you can concentrate on writing?
- Do you need a developer to manage the technical parts of your website?

I paid a designer to create a cover for this book. I could have designed the cover myself, but the results wouldn't have been as professional, and my time is better spent writing.

Similarly, I know a successful blogger who writes outlines for his posts. He gives these outlines to an editor to complete and format in WordPress. The blogger says writing like this enables him to finish up to eight blog posts per week.

The longer you work on a piece, the harder it is to see your mistakes and figure out if you have gone astray. What's interesting to you might not be interesting to the reader.

If you haven't talked to any readers, then how can you know?

Friends and family, if they will be honest with you, are a good start. They can help proofread your work and offer advice on how to improve. Or you could ask colleagues to check if your copy is getting the job done.

If your friends or colleagues are any good, they'll come back with suggestions for words and ideas you can remove, include or rework. They'll probably pick up a few typos that you missed too.

Don't expose your unedited writing in all its ugliness to the world. Get help now before it's too late.

VALUE FEEDBACK

If you write, you must seek out feedback.

I was a member of a creative writing and non-fiction writing group in Dublin for several years.

They hated almost everything I wrote.

These more accomplished writers told me how I could improve my work. So I listened.

Other more accomplished writers expose you to new kinds of writing and new ways of looking at your work. They encourage and push you to write beyond anything you've attempted before.

You could join a writing group in your community or a critique group online. Non-fiction writers can join numerous professional online writing courses and communities too.

Not every writer needs to join a writing critique group, however.

I interviewed famous Irish novelist Jennifer Johnston several years ago. Since 1972, she has published more than 20 books and numerous plays. Johnston told me she has little time for creative writing groups.

"They take you away from your work," she said. "I didn't need them."

Johnston didn't need a writing group, but she is an exception. Her father Denis was a famous playwright. He provided his daughter with the feedback she needed to improve.

Unless you're Johnston or you've someone like Denis who can review your work, joining a writing group is beneficial. Your participation encourages accountability, and it opens you up to criticism. You also get to spend time in the company of other writers and learn from their experiences.

Not everything these people have to say will be correct or

of value, just like not everything you write will succeed or have merit.

Finding this out is half the fun.

FIND YOUR MENTOR

Do you have a mentor for your writing?

Finding a mentor who knows more about writing than you do is a shortcut to better prose. I've met several people who helped me improve my writing.

A tutor in university explained how to write for an academic audience. The instructor of a creative writing showed the students and me how to improve our prose and kill our darlings.

An English teacher taught me how to bend any topic towards an idea that I wanted to write about. And an editor I didn't get along with demonstrated how to write clearly and without obvious bias.

Some of these people knew they were mentoring me; some of them didn't.

I never met one of my mentors. His name was John Cheever, and he died in 1982, one year after I was born.

So, how can John Cheever be my mentor?

Several years ago, I considered abandoning writing altogether. My freelance contracts had dried up, I'd received multiple rejection letters from various competitions and editors, and my writing was rotting in my drawer.

Then I discovered *The Journals of John Cheever*. I'd read some of Cheever's short stories before, but his journals are a different beast entirely.

In his journals, Cheever wrote about his personal demons and his journey towards becoming an accomplished writer. Through reading his works, I rediscovered my passion for writing, and I found a reason to keep going.

Even today, when I become disillusioned with writing, I think of Cheever's mantra that a "good page of prose remains invincible".

I think of him writing day after day through a difficult marriage, alcoholism, depression, being a parent, happiness and success.

No matter what, Cheever wrote.

MODEL YOUR MENTORS

Another great way to get the most from your mentor or an expert you admire deeply is to apply as many of their practices as possible. This process is called **modelling**, and it will help you achieve mastery faster.

In his book *Mastery*, Robert Greene explains how this process works:

> The key then to attaining this higher level of intelligence is to make our years of study qualitatively rich. We don't simply absorb information - we internalise it and make it our own by finding some way to put this knowledge to practical use.

By modelling your creative betters, you can avoid many of the mistakes your mentors made on their way to success and save time because they will have done the hard work of sifting through good and bad information for you.

No, I'm not advocating you steal your mentor's work. Instead, figure out a way to get close to your creative hero and learn from them ethically.

Today, many creators and writers offer online courses and coaching classes. When you sign up, they will teach you what they know. If this isn't possible, read as much of their work as you can get your hands on.

Whatever your approach, absorb and implement as many lessons as you can from your mentor(s).

To avoid becoming overwhelmed, focus on learning only from one or two mentors at a time. Then when you've learnt or applied as many of their lessons as you can, find your next mentor.

HANDLE CRITICISM LIKE A PRO

The first time I wrote an article for a newspaper my editor hated it. He told me he wasn't going to publish my work.

"If you don't improve your writing, I'm going to fire you," he said.

I went into the bathroom and thought about quitting. What kind of person was I? Was I lazy and incompetent? Did I deserve to be fired?

Until this point, everybody had told me I could write. My identity was intimately connected with the idea of being a writer and if an accomplished writer like my editor hated my work, then who was I?

The first time I submitted a short story to a creative writing group, the instructor of the group announced to the class that my story reminded him of a hammy B-movie.

"You need to spend more time writing something we can believe in," he said.

I went home and tore up the next short story I was working on. What was the point in wasting so much time working on a story only for another person to hate it?

Perhaps my nights were better spent watching television.

It took time, but I accepted their criticisms. They were right. My article was terrible and my short stories were stuffed with clichés. I vowed to try harder. I promised myself I'd improve.

Now I seek criticisms out. Praise is useful but negative

feedback is more valuable. It gives the productive writer a chance to expose a fault in their craft and fix it.

Some criticism might be constructive, and some of it won't help at all. But your fiercest critics could become your biggest enablers for better writing.

My favourite story of a writer embracing criticism involves social media guru and business author Gary Vaynerchuk. He read each of the one-star and two-star reviews of his book *Crush It* on Amazon – always a disconcerting experience for an author – and replied to them.

One of Vaynerchuk's comments said,

> Frank. I am so so sorry I under delivered for you, I hope to meet u and spend 15 minutes apologizing and answering any questions u may have, I guess I needed more details in there for u, I am so sorry.

A critical reviewer Vaynerchuk replied too was impressed. He wrote,

> Gary, I still don't agree with you, but I so appreciate the time you took to reach out to me and understand where I was coming from.

The next time you finish what you're working on, seek out criticism. Ask your friends, your family and your enemies to tell you what they love and hate about your work. Like Vaynerchuk, don't let the bad reviews get you down.

Use feedback to become a better, stronger, more accomplished writer.

LEARN WHEN TO EDIT

"If it sounds like writing, I rewrite it." – Elmore Leonard

You spent hours working on your article or book chapter.

You gathered up fresh ideas, researched your arguments meticulously, and put hours in the chair. The work paid off too.

You got the words out of your head and onto the blank page and now, finally, you've finished writing your first draft.

Or have you?

When you read through your draft, something terrible happens.

You know deep down it's not very good. Those ideas you thought were great don't quite hold up. There are gaps in the research and the writing.

Ugh.

Now, you're unsure what to do, and a deadline is looming like a guillotine.

How are you going to take this messy first draft and turn it into something you can serve up to your readers?

If you've ever struggled with these kinds of problems, you are not alone.

SEPARATE WRITING AND EDITING

Writing is the process of getting ideas out of your head and onto the blank page, telling stories and communicating through the written word.

Editing is the process of reviewing, arranging and polishing your writing so readers understand and enjoy what you're saying.

Whether you write fiction or non-fiction, they are two distinct activities demanding different skill sets.

The secret to productive writing is editing your work after you finish writing a messy first draft. To do both at once is to indulge in the myth of multitasking. (See chapter 28).

To edit productively, you must be able to zoom out from your writing and consider it as a whole.

This just isn't possible if you're still trying to hit a word count or produce an early draft.

So when you finish a draft, let it in your computer or on your desk for a day or two, or at least long enough so that the writing doesn't feel so fresh (see chapter 29).

For this reason, many successful authors write drafts early in the morning and edit them in the afternoon, taking care to space out both activities. Or they hire an editor to prepare their work for publication.

FOCUS ON EDITING

Editing your first draft is more important than obsessing about finding the right tools.

So by all means use the "Track Changes" feature in Word or Google Docs if they work for you.

Your editing tool of choice should enable you to restore earlier drafts of your article in case your changes don't work.

That said, while employed as a print journalist, I learned several self-editing tricks.

My colleagues often printed at least one draft of their articles.

Then, they turned their computer screens off and read through this draft, marking up the pages with a red pen.

I asked my editor, "Why?" and he said:

"Paper is less distracting than a computer, and it forces you to concentrate on the flow of your ideas."

Now, before you print out your draft, change the font of your document to a monospaced font like Courier and the line spacing to double. This way, your eye will spot issues easily.

The formatting changes offers space to write your edits with red pen in between sentences and along the margins.

Then, all you need is some paper and a quiet place to work.

Editing a Print Out of a First Draft

KEEP YOUR CUTOFFS

Where do your unpublished blog posts and articles, leftover research and abandoned chapters go?

The productive writer keeps them in a digital or paper file where he or she can refer to them. These abandoned ideas might not belong in the writer's current writing project, but he or she will find a future opportunity to turn cutoffs into rounded, usable ideas.

Relying on your cutoffs isn't a shortcut, and it's not cheating. Let no one tell you otherwise.

If a cook can reuse ingredients for another meal and a technician can reuse computer parts, why can't a writer return to his or her abandoned ideas?

Writers shouldn't have to reinvent themselves every time they are presented with a new writing project. If we did that, we wouldn't have time to finish anything.

Not everything you discard will be of merit, but why take

the chance of letting a semi-formed idea disappear into the ether?

If you researched a topic only to find you couldn't use what you found, you could always draw on this research for your next project.

Or if you've argued a point only to edit it out entirely, you can use parts of your argument in a future article, blog post or chapter.

Keeping your cuttings is one way to overcome writer's block and advance troublesome projects because instead of staring at a blank page, you can peruse your old musings.

Sometimes I take an abandoned idea and use it as a jumping-off point, or a writing prompt, for something new. (See chapter 3).

I've written dozens of blog posts that were never published, and I've interviewed many people only to set aside large portions of what they had to say.

In both cases, I've used extracts from my abandoned blog posts and interview transcripts for new writing projects.

Even if you never use your cutoffs, they don't represent wasted time or energy.

Instead, consider them markers on the path towards a more polished and coherent work. For a productive writer, nothing is ever lost or wasted.

EDIT AND THEN EDIT SOME MORE

So what should you do if you've spent hours editing a second or third draft, but it's not quite right?

There's a good chance you've reached the point of diminishing returns.

At this stage, getting help is the only way you'll improve your draft.

Consider the curious case of author and entrepreneur James Altucher.

He presented a version of a near-final manuscript of his 2013 book *Choose Yourself* to marketer, editor and writer Ryan Holiday.

Altucher wanted Ryan to help him with an aggressive marketing plan to promote *Choose Yourself.*

Instead, Ryan insisted on sixteen more rounds of edits over the following six months including a restructuring of the book, the removal of four chapters and the addition of two more.

In the end, *Choose Yourself* sold more than 600,000 copies and USA Today called it one of the 12 best business books of all time.

GET HELP

Books require more rounds of editing than articles. So if you want your writing to succeed, it pays to enlist the help of your peers.

In his 2017 book *Perennial Seller: The Art of Making and Marketing Work that Lasts,* Holiday explained,

> "Nobody creates flawless first drafts. And nobody creates better second drafts without the intervention of someone else. Nobody."

Send your later drafts to your editor for critical feedback and explain where you're stuck.

He or she might be able to give you a fresh angle or point out what to remove or expand on.

You can also use professional editorial services to improve your work. At the back of this book, I've included some resources for finding an editor.

Alternatively, give the draft to an early reader or close family member and ask them to be honest about what works and doesn't work.

Learning how and when to edit, like cooking, takes practice. So put your time in, and your readers will keep coming back for more.

GET OVER YOUR FAILURES

"Whenever a thing is done for the first time, it releases a little demon." – Emily Dickinson

If you want to become a more productive writer, accept you're going to fail time and again.

I've written dozens of blog posts and articles nobody read. Editors rejected ideas I pitched. I've published articles only to find they contained typos or factual errors. I've also spent hours preparing stories and articles for competitions only to find they weren't even long-listed.

Each one of these failures hurt and, at times, I questioned what I was doing.

However, my collection of failures gave me the opportunity to improve my writing. On the occasions when I passed up these opportunities, I met with the same failures weeks or months later.

Failing is part of the writing process. This little demon is a sign that you turned up and tried. Just ask Cheever, Melville or Dickinson.

LEARN FROM OTHERS

Some writers and artists say they can't bear to look at their old work, and once they're done with something, they never want to see it again.

Before he died, Cheever told *The Paris Review* he felt a "sense of clinical fatigue" after finishing a novel.

Despite the success of his short stories, he described having little time for many of them after they were published.

"I love them, but I can't read them; in many cases, I wouldn't love them any longer if I did," he said in 1969.

Hundreds of writers became successful only after their death.

For example, many critics cite *Moby-Dick* as one of the greatest works of all time, but Herman Melville didn't live to enjoy the book's acclaim.

Emily Dickinson struggled for much of her life to find anyone who would print her work. She famously received this rejection letter from a publisher:

> Your poems are quite as remarkable for defects as for beauties and are generally devoid of true poetical qualities.

Rejection and failure hurt, but they didn't stop these writers and they shouldn't stop you.

LEAVE YOUR DEMONS BEHIND

As I progressed from one media organisation to the next, I built a portfolio of articles, news stories and clippings that I was proud of. I cut out these clippings and stored them carefully in an expensive leather case.

I told myself this portfolio was for potential employers. It was my insurance policy against future unemployment, and I believed that every accomplished journalist kept these portfolios.

Witness my exercise in vanity.

By keeping this portfolio, I was holding onto past successes. I was telling myself I didn't need to move forward as a writer because "Look! I've already been published in a national newspaper. Surely I'm good enough."

I wasn't good enough. Many of my articles were badly written or poorly researched. Part of me knew this, but in keeping my portfolio I was holding onto failures.

My clippings reminded me of missed opportunities. I thought of promising jobs that came to an abrupt end and of stories that felt important at the time but meant nothing weeks or months later. I couldn't live like that. Something had to change.

One Saturday morning, I gathered old boxes, broken appliances, empty paint cans and my portfolio. I put them in the car, and I drove to the dump. I threw everything into the skips.

Keeping this portfolio was holding me back from seeing new opportunities, such as a college course I wanted to take and later a blog that I wanted to start.

After throwing away my old clippings and articles, I felt empty; but like an empty vessel, I was ready for something new.

I was able to go home and consider how I was going to make a living from writing without trying to become a successful journalist. I was able to fall forwards.

REFRAME YOUR SETBACKS

Like the runner who falls while training, a writer must get back up again after failing.

The only other option is stopping altogether, and that's not a realistic choice for anyone who is passionate about the written word.

So write about your failures and how they've shaped who you are. Explain how your setbacks helped you become the person you are today. Describe how you overcame some failures and learnt to live with others.

I'm not advocating wallowing in failure. Instead, reframe your setbacks as learning experiences.

Ask yourself:

- Do your older articles (the ones you're proud of) add value to your writing career today?
- Are you holding onto the past?
- Can you explore writing in a new genre?
- Could a writing teacher or coach help you get over this plateau?
- What does success look like in a month, a year or five years?
- Who has already accomplished what you want to do?

Perhaps you lack the skills to achieve what you want with your writing. Then, improve by taking a class, online or otherwise.

Maybe you need to spend more time building relationships with your readers or editors. Then, study marketing and spend time getting to know who you're writing for (you could speak to a reader over Skype for 30-minutes).

Or you could simply need to put more time into

improving the quality of your work. Then, commit to spending twice as long on your next piece of writing.

Remember, you're better off trying and failing, falling forwards and learning what you can from painful experiences than sitting on the couch and doing nothing.

FINISH WHAT YOU STARTED

"Most people have dozens of things that they need to do to make progress on many fronts, but they don't yet know what they are." – David Allen

When was the last time you took 30 minutes out from your week to review how your writing is going?

Would you like to see how your writing is progressing?

How can you figure out what you need to write next and what you should stop working on?

A simple strategy can help you answer these questions and gain some control over your writing – the weekly review.

I learnt about the weekly review several years ago from David Allen, author of *Getting Things Done*.

It's a strategy for business people and professionals to take charge of their lives. This strategy is also useful for writers who want to accomplish more faster.

Since putting this strategy into practice, I've found it to

be a great way of taking charge of my writing and other areas of my life.

The weekly review gives me confidence that I'm working on the right things at the right time, and it helps me shine a light on neglected parts of my creative or writing life.

The good news is implementing a weekly review, and this final strategy doesn't take a lot of time or extra work.

HOLD A WEEKLY REVIEW

At the end of the week, put aside 30 to 60 minutes for your review. If it's helpful, book this time in your calendar as a recurring appointment and make a commitment to keep it.

Use this time to stop writing, zoom out and gain some perspective on your work.

The goal of your weekly review is to figure out what you accomplished over the past few days, what you overlooked and what you need to do or write next.

During your review, be honest with yourself. Ask and answer questions like:

- What did I accomplish or write this week?
- What went well/didn't go well?
- What are my most important task(s) for next week?
- What was my word count for the week?
- How many hours did I spend writing?
- How many ideas did I generate?
- How did I market my writing or my work?
- What events or deadlines are in my calendar for the previous/next seven days that I need to act on?
- What have I been putting off?
- What should I stop doing or say no to?

BRYAN COLLINS

Remember, this review is not the time for working on your projects or writing.

Use your weekly review to clarify your priorities and make plans for future writing projects. This might mean adding missing activities or upcoming deadlines to your calendar or deciding if you need to renegotiate commitments with your editor or clients.

If you use a To Do list, this is the time to update it with new items and remove old items you have no intention of completing.

You can ask and answer these questions in a journal if you like. When you've answered these questions and you're clear about what you need to do next, you'll be able to hit the blank page feeling better about yourself and your work.

During the weekly review, I file my research, organise my notes and quickly read through the ideas I came up with during the week. This helps me evaluate if there's anything I've overlooked or if there's an idea I can use over the coming days in my work.

I also write down or mark minor accomplishments during the week such as hitting a target word count or completing a book chapter. These minor creative accomplishments are important to mark and a great way to boost your motivation.

Think of it this way: Paragraphs make up book chapters, and finished chapters will fill a book. In other words, the accumulation of minor achievements contributes to a major accomplishment.

The weekly review is a powerful productive strategy, which if used correctly, will help you plan for future writing projects secure in the knowledge that you have the resources and time to finish what you started.

DISCOVER WHAT LIES AHEAD

Finishing what you started writing isn't so tough now that you know how to manage your time and commitments. Once you get into the habit of finishing, the rewards are immense. You'll get:

Your hands dirty: Studying the work habits and creative strategies of writers like Hemingway and the ad copywriter Caples is fun, but writing isn't a spectator sport. You'll learn more of this craft by wading in up to your neck.

Learning opportunities: If you ship your work and it's badly received, you can use this feedback to become a better writer. If you don't ship, you won't get feedback, and you'll never get a chance to improve.

Smarter: Finishing a piece trains your brain to make new connections and come up with better ideas for your next writing project.

Answers: Are you a non-fiction writer, a copywriter, a story-teller or a non-fiction writer? Finishing your work will help you answer these questions because you'll know more of what you enjoy and what you're good at.

Over blindspots: Do you have trouble writing strong introductions? What can you do to write better headlines? How can you deepen your research? Treasure the difficult moments; they are the foundations of your writing practice.

Faster: You're an athlete and writing is a race. It might be a sprint, a 10-mile event or a marathon. Whatever the length of your work, get through it and you'll finish the next one faster.

More confident: When your article appears in print, your short story in a magazine or your blog post on a popular site, you'll feel lighter than you have in months. Then when you sit down to write again, you'll be hungry for more success.

A free education: If you guest post for a popular website, you'll have the chance to talk to another editor who can help you improve your work and (if the relationship goes well) provide you with opportunities for future work. Some writers pay money for this kind of feedback.

Paid: Professional writers turn up, they do the work, and they move on. They get paid. You deserve to get paid too.

BECOME THE PRODUCTIVE WRITER

Now that you've digested the 33 productivity strategies in this book, you know writing will always feel like a messy and sometimes disjointed pursuit. It doesn't fit neatly into any box or to do list.

That doesn't mean you can get away with missing deadlines and permanently unfinished projects. These are the hallmarks of amateurs who don't know where they're going or what they're doing. If you made it this far, you're not an amateur.

Several years ago, I was an amateur (albeit one who had convinced some people otherwise).

I worked as a journalist for a local newspaper in Ireland. I had to write news stories each week, cover council meetings, political speeches and business stories in the area.

This was my first real job since graduating college, and I saw it as my big break into the big, bad, wide world of print journalism.

For a man with such ambitions for his career, I had one big problem.

I spent more time talking to people in the office, reading

the news online and doing anything but my job. Eventually, my procrastination caught up with me.

One sunny Wednesday morning, after I'd missed a big deadline the night before, my editor called me into the office. He told me to close the door and take a seat. You know it's not good when they tell you to take a seat.

"I'm not happy with your progress here Bryan, you're letting things slip," he said leaning back in his chair. "The reality is if you can't finish the damn thing, you're not doing your job, and if you're not doing your job, this newspaper will have to let you go."

"I can do better, I can explain," I said. "Give me another chance."

I didn't deserve another chance, and I had no genuine excuses. My editor was right. I wasn't doing my job. Luckily, he didn't fire me (at least not that day).

Since then, I've made every possible mistake writing fiction and non-fiction. I've learnt the hard way that finishing something, anything, gives a writer the confidence to write again.

If you can't finish the damn thing, you're not doing your job. You're not fulfilling the challenge productive writers like Stephen King laid down for the rest of us.

Ask yourself:

- What's the last writing project you abandoned?
- When was the last time you published or submitted a writing project for publication?
- Are you constantly seeking new ways to get feedback about your writing?
- When will you finish what you're writing?
- Why are you procrastinating?

If you finish what you are working on, you will feel a

sense of accomplishment alien to the writer who gave up altogether. Creating, writing and finishing your work will teach you far more than polishing pages of prose for months on end.

Whether you're writing fiction or non-fiction, shipping is more important than perfection. Instead of abandoning a writing project or slaving away indefinitely, set a target for submission or publication.

Stick to this target, and if you miss it, finish, publish or submit your work as soon as you can.

Don't ship mediocrity or publish a writing project for the sake of it. Conversely, don't let your writing stagnate in a drawer.

Confidence comes when you reach the end.

When you finish your next writing project, some people might criticise or reject your work. They could be right, but you still gain a victory.

Even if your writing project is a failure, at least you will be free to write something else, something better.

I've finished a lot of awful articles in my time, but finishing gave me the confidence to see the writing process through.

Afterwards, I was able to show people my work (warts and all) and learn from their feedback, which is invaluable. It's your chance to learn how to become a better writer for free.

If you get into the habit of finishing your work, you can become a writer who thinks of an idea, fleshes it out, edits, rewrites, polishes and then rewrites some more, before finishing the damn thing.

None of this is possible if you get hung up on creating the perfect piece of writing.

My editor and I long since fell out, but I'm still writing. Are you?

WHAT ARE YOU WAITING FOR?

Y ou must know that words are all you need to succeed. In the wrong hands, they can become weapons to tear down others. In the right hands, they are a salve for the boredom, frustration and pain around you.

If you are lonely or depressed, if your wife or husband has left you, if you are broke or greedy, if you are hungry for success or sick of your ambitions, if you are on a creative high or stuck in rut, if you know who you are or if you've outgrown your ambitions, whoever you want to be, *you must write*.

Writing is hard. Every writer will tell you a battle wages between us and a finished work.

Pressfield, author of *The War of Art*, explains we writers have to slay our dragons on the page:

> We're facing dragons too. Fire-breathing griffins of the soul, whom we must outfight and outwit to reach the treasure of our self-in-potential to release the maiden who is God's plan and destiny for ourselves and the answer to why we were put on this planet.

Go now from this book and sit in a quiet room and face your dragons. Put one word after another on the blank page. Your sentences will make you feel sick. The awfulness of their construction will wound you.

Your head will spin, and you will look outside and wonder how else to spend your time. Then when you're ready to quit, a great thing will happen.

You will write one true sentence.

You will create something meaningful and reinvent yourself.

This is how you will leave a mark on your world, however small.

I apologise because I deceived you.

This book isn't a guide for more creative or productive writing. This book is my *Manifesto for Writing*.

What's yours?

THE END IS NEAR

Now that we've reached the end of *The Savvy Writer's Guide to Productivity*, I need your help. I need you to share some of your expert knowledge with me so I can improve my work.

If you have any suggestions for improving this book, please contact me by emailing bryan@becomeawriterto-day.com.

On http://becomeawritertoday.com, you can find out why I'm obsessed with the written word. You'll also receive insider articles and an email course that will help you write faster.

Together, we can become better writers.

TOOLS FOR BECOMING A MORE
PRODUCTIVE WRITER

Below is a list of tools I use and rely on as an author and blogger.

I've also included some other recommended resources that will help you become a more productive writer.

The list is relatively long and, depending on what you write, you won't need to use all of these tools. Remember, writing is important than any tool.

For an always up-to-date list of these tools, please visit https://becomeawritertoday.com/writing-apps/

99designs

In the past, I've used 99designs to find a designer to create a book cover for one of my books.

If you want a professional design (like a logo, t-shirt, business card or packaging) for your online business, 99designs is a good place to start. See https://becomeawritertoday.com/99designs-competition/

A smartphone

The best camera is the one you have with you at the time, and if you need to take a picture or just capture an idea, your smartphone is almost always the best choice. I use an iPhone.

A whiteboard

I keep a large whiteboard next to where I write. It's a great way of capturing and organising ideas. I also use it for mind maps and for creating outlines for articles, chapters and even books. I find a whiteboard less confining that traditional digital tools.

Audible

As a writer, your inputs (what you read, listen to and watch) are just as important as your outputs (what you write, paint or draw). I spend at least an hour a day listening to audiobooks that I purchased from Audible on my smartphone.

If you sign up, they'll give you your first audiobook for free. To learn more about creating your audiobook, please see https://becomeawritertoday.com/how-to-make-an-audiobook/

Behance

A showcase site for design and other creative work. Behance is great for inspiration and also for finding designers to work with. Also, see Dribble.

Brain.FM

Brain.FM provides AI-generated music for focus, relaxation and deep work. When I use this, I find I can enter a state of creative flow faster. Plug in a pair of headphones and you're good to go.

Buffer

I use Buffer to share articles, photos and social media updates by myself and others on Instagram, Facebook, LinkedIn, Twitter and Pinterest. Buffer simplifies sharing social media updates across multiple networks and enables you to schedule your updates in advance.

You can also collaborate with others and enable them to manage your social media profiles... leaving you more time to work on your creative projects. More advanced social media users should consider Meet Edgar.

Canva

For years, I used Photoshop and the rest of the Adobe Suite to create images. Today, I rely on Canva because it simplifies creating images using a drag-and-drop editor.

Creative Commons

This site – https://creativecommons.org/ –will help you legally share your work online and find a license or copyright that suits your business model, website or project.

You can also find images, music and other media that you can use in your writing projects, commercial or otherwise.

Nuance Dragon Naturally Speaking

I use dictation software to dictate early drafts of blog posts, book chapters and articles. This piece of software enables me to write faster, and it also reduces the amount of time I spend struggling with repetitive strain injury (RSI). In this article, I explain how to get started with dictation http://becomeawritertoday.com/speech-to-text

Evernote

If I have an idea that I don't want to forget, I keep it in here. I also save articles I like into Evernote as part of my personal swipe file. Sometimes, I take photos of mind maps on my whiteboard with my phone and put them in Evernote too. It's my digital brain.

Image sites

Gratisography contains awesome and free high-resolution photos you can use for your creative projects, as does All The Free Stock and Death to the Stock.

I recommend Depositphotos for premium stock images. You could also take the images yourself and apply an Instagram filter. Designers can get icons on The Noun Project.

Freedom

If you keep getting distracted while writing, use the app Freedom. It will disable your internet access for a pre-determined period, allowing you to focus on writing and not on cat videos!

Grammarly

If you need help proofing your work, I always recommend you hire a proofreader. However, I also recommend Grammarly as another line of defence and for checking your writing as you go. See https://becomeawritertoday.com/grammar-checker-review-grammarly/

Google Docs

I use Google Docs to write on the go and to track my progress in spreadsheets. I also collaborate with other writers and creative professionals, and *it's free*.

G Suite

It's time to put the hard-drives and USB keys away. Essentially, G Suite enables me to send and receive emails from the becomeawritertoday.com domain (bryan[at]Become-AWriterToday.com) using the Gmail interface.

I also get lots of additional cloud storage and can easily collaborate with other writers, editors and designers. This isn't free, but it's affordable.

Headline Analyzer

This free online tool will check your headlines and give you practical tips for improving them so they are more emotional and captivating. Alternatively, consider CoSchedule Headline Analyzer.

Headspace

This is my meditation app of choice. If you've never meditated before, Andy Puddicombe will teach you the basics through guided lessons. I also suggest searching for Tara Brach's free guided meditations online.

Hemingway App

If you're not a confident writer, don't worry. Hemingway App will review your text and, in the spirit of Ernest

Hemingway, it will tell you what to remove or edit so your writing is bold and clear.

Kibin

Unlike many proofreading and editing services, Kibin will edit for grammar, spelling, punctuation, sentence structure and more. I've sent book chapters and articles to this service. See http://kibin.com

Kindle Spy

KindleSpy is a great tool that will help you see which books are selling on Amazon and how much they earn. It saves time on keyword research, and you can use this information to increase sales of your book.

LeadPages

I use LeadPages to create landing and squeeze pages for my books. I also use it to create sign-up forms for my mailing list. See https://becomeawritertoday.com/leadpages-review/

Your bed or chair of choice

Fact: Napping is conducive to creativity. Just ask Salvador Dali. The trick is to wake yourself up after 20 minutes so you avoid going into a deep sleep. Then when you wake, get straight to work.

Noise cancelling headphones and an album of instrumental music

A good set of noise cancelling headphones will help you concentrate on your work no matter where you are. Each morning, I don my pair and listen to albums like "Rain for Sleeping and Relaxation" on repeat while I write.

(Yes, that album is exactly like the name sounds.)

iMindMap/MindNode/MindMeister

I've used these affordable tools to create mind maps in the past. They're easy to learn too. Alternatively, you can create a mind map using pen and paper. To see how I use

mindmaps   for   writing,   visit
https://becomeawritertoday.com/mind-mapping/

Medium

Do you just want to write and share your ideas online, but you're not interested in running a blog? Medium removes all of the technical challenges of blogging and helps you connect with readers.

Pilot G4 Pen and a Moleskine notebook

No, there's no need to use a Moleskine notebook for writing or capturing ideas, but I'm drawn to the build quality of these notebooks and the feel of the paper. I've a box full of these near where I write.

Even if you're not drawn to these admittedly expensive notebooks, working on your ideas with a pen (you can't go wrong with the Pilot G4) and paper will liberate fresh thinking.

Reedsy

If you want to find a book editor, proof-reader or cover designer, Reedsy takes the hassle out of it. When you sign up, you get access to a community of self-publishing profes-sionals that are ready to work with you and on your book. See http://reedsy.com

Screenflow for Mac

This is a great tool for recording video and screencasts. It's also relatively simple to edit your recordings and export them to a format suitable for Facebook, YouTube or your website. Also consider Camtasia.

Scrivener

I can't recommend Scrivener enough. I use it to write blog posts and books. I've used Scrivener to write feature articles for newspapers, reports, a thesis and books. Other useful writing apps include Ulysses, Pages and IA Writer. Get my   free   Scrivener   blogging   template   at http://becomeawritertoday.com/using-scrivener-blogging-ultimate-guide/

Sumo

Sumo is an all-in-one tool that enables you to gather email addresses, set up a share bar on the side of blog posts and also track how people interact with your work online.

If you're sharing your work online, I highly recommended it. See https://becomeawritertoday.com/sumome-review/

Upwork

No matter how talented or hard-working you are, it's impossible to do everything alone. UpWork is a great service for finding designers, editors and more who can help you with time-consuming tasks so you can spend more time on your book.

I've used Upwork to hire video-editors and developers who fixed problems on my website.

Web-hosting

For your author website or blog, I suggest hosting with Siteground. If you need help, check out my detailed guide on how to start a blog: https://becomeawritertoday.com/start-a-blog/

REMEMBER YOUR BONUS

I created a **FREE video masterclass** that will help cut months off how long it takes you to write your book by using my best tactics and strategies.

DID YOU CLAIM YOUR FREE BONUS?

VISIT
becomeawritertoday.com/author

If you want to get this masterclass today, please visit http://becomeawritertoday.com/author

BECOME A WRITER TODAY

Yes, You Can Write!
101 Proven Writing Prompts that Will Help You Find
Creative Ideas Faster for Your Journal, Blogging, Writing
Your Book and More
(Book 1)

The Savvy Writer's Guide to Productivity
How to Work Less, Finish Writing Your Story or Book, and
Find the Success You Deserve
(Book 2)

The Art of Writing a Non-Fiction Book
An Easy Guide to Researching, Creating, Editing, and Self-
publishing Your First Book
(Book 3)

http://becomeawritertodaybook.com

THE POWER OF CREATIVITY

Learning How to Build Lasting Habits, Face Your Fears and
Change Your Life
(Book 1)

An Uncommon Guide to Mastering Your Inner Genius and
Finding New Ideas That Matter
(Book 2)

How to Conquer Procrastination, Finish Your Work and
Find Success
(Book 3)

http://thepowerofcreativitybook.com

ABOUT THE AUTHOR

In this life, Bryan Collins is an author.

In another life, he worked as a journalist and radio producer. Before that, he plucked chickens. He is passionate about helping people accomplish more with their writing projects, and when he's not writing, he's running.

At becomeawritertoday.com, Bryan offers new writers practical advice about writing, creativity, productivity and more. His work has appeared on *Fast Company*, *Lifehacker* and *Copyblogger*.

Bryan holds a degree in communications and journalism, a diploma in social care, a master's degree in disability studies and a diploma in digital media.

You can reach him on Twitter @BryanJCollins, via email at bryan@becomeawritertoday.com or join his Become a Writer Today Facebook page.

Bryan is also the author of the novella *Poor Brother, Rich Brother* and a three-part series *The Power of Creativity*.

He lives an hour outside of Dublin.

becomeawritertoday.com
bryan@becomeawritertoday.com

AN ASK

I wrote, published and marketed *The Savvy Writer's Guide to Productivity* because I'm passionate about what I do and our craft.

So if you enjoyed this book or found it helpful in any way, take a moment to **write a short review** on Goodreads or Amazon.

Your reviews mean more people will find and buy my book. Your reviews also mean I can publish more books like this one.

Thank you for spending time reading my work.

For A.

The Savvy Writer's Guide to Productivity:
How to Work Less, Finish Writing Your Story or Book,
and Find the Success You Deserve
Fourth Edition

This book was previously titled
A Handbook for the Productive Writer:
33 Ways You Can Finish What You Started

Become a Writer Today

REFERENCES

Books

Altucher, James. *Choose Yourself*. 2013.

Allen, David. *Getting Things Done*. 2011.

Austen, Jane. *Pride and Prejudice*. 1992.

Babauta, Leo. *The Power of Less*. 2009.

Brown, Christy. *Down All the Days*. 1990.

Brown, Christy. *My Left Foot*. 1990.

Carnegie, Dale. *How to Win Friends and Influence People*. 1998.

Cheever, John. *The Journals*. 2011.

Covey, Stephen R. *The Seven Habits of Highly Effective People*. 2013.

Currey, Mason. *Daily Rituals: How Artists Work*. 2013.

Dickens, Charles. *A Tale of Two Cities*. 2011.

Doyle, Roddy. *The Commitments*. 2010

Doyle, Roddy. *The Snapper*. 2008.

Fitzgerald, F. Scott. *The Great Gatsby*. 2013.

Franzen, Jonathan. *The Corrections*. 2010.

Gelb, Michael J. *How to Think Like Leonardo da Vinci*. 2000.

Holiday, Ryan. *Perennial Seller: The Art of Making and Marketing Work that Lasts*. Profile Books. Kindle Edition. 2017.

Isaacson, Walter. *Einstein: His Life and Universe*. 2008.

Isaacson, Walter. *Steve Jobs: The Exclusive Biography*. 2011.

Joyce, James. *Ulysses*. 2012.

Kafka, Franz. *Metamorphosis*. 2009.

Kennedy, Dan S. *The Ultimate Sales Letter: Attract New Customers and Boost Your Sales* (4th Ed). 2011.

King, Stephen. *On Writing: A Memoir of the Craft*. 2010.

Murakami, Haruki. *What I Talk About When I Talk About Running*. 2011.

Kleon, Austin. *Steal Like An Artist: 10 Things Nobody Told You About Being Creative*. 2012.

McKeown, Greg. *Essentialism: The Disciplined Pursuit of Less. 2014.*

Levy, Mark. *Accidental Genius: Using Writing to Generate Your Best Ideas, Insight and Content* (2nd Ed). 2009.

Nabokov, Vladimir. *Lolita*. 2012.

Pressfield, Steven and Coyne, Sean. *The War of Art*. 2011.

Plath, Sylvia. *The Bell Jar*. 2005.

McKee, Robert. *Story: Substance, Structure Style and The Principles of Screenwriting*. 1997.

Melville, Herman. *Moby-Dick*. 2014.

Orwell, George. *1984*. 2013.

Platt, Sean. Truant, Johnny B. Wright. *Write. Publish. Repeat. The No-Luck Required Guide to Self-Publishing Success*. 2013.

Salinger, J.D. *The Catcher in the Rye*. 2014.

Suzuki, Shunryu. *Zen Mind, Beginner's Mind*. 2011.

Tolstoy, Leo. *Anna Karenina*. 2012.

Vaynerchuk, Gary. *The Thank You Economy*. 2011.

Vaynerchuk, Gary. *Crushing It!: How Great Entrepreneurs*

Build Their Business and Influence & and How You Can, Too. HarperCollins. Kindle Edition. 2018.

Woolf, Virginia. *A Writer's Diary (1918-1941)*. 2013.

Zinsser, William. *On Writing Well*. 2006.

Articles and Online Resources

80Pct Solutions. Freedom. 2014. https://macfreedom.com/

Altucher, James. The James Altucher Podcast: Episode 17: "Chris Brogan: Are You a Freak?". 2014.

Björk, Johanna. "Benjamin Franklin's Routine: Do Good Each Day". 2013. Taken from http://www.goodlifer.com/2013/02/benjamin-franklins-routine-do-good-each-day/ on July 4, 2014.

Burrell, Diana. "Renegade Writer Q&A David Allen". Taken from http://www.therenegadewriter.com/2007/03/19/renegade-writer-qa-david-allen/ on June 24, 2014. Renegade Writer.

Chrisafis, Angelique. "Overlong, overrated and unmoving: Roddy Doyle's verdict on James Joyce's Ulysses". 2004. Take from http://www.theguardian.com/uk/2004/feb/10/booksnews.ireland on June 21, 2014. The Guardian.

Colzato, Lorenza S. Ayca, Ozturk. Hommel, Bernhard. "Meditate to create: the impact of focused-attention and open-monitoring training on convergent and divergent thinking". 2012. Taken from http://journal.frontiersin.org/Journal/10.3389/fpsyg.2012.00116/full on July 2, 2014. Leiden University.

Conradt, Stacy. "Vladamir Nabokov Talks Synesthesia". 2013. Taken from http://mentalfloss.com/article/49442/vladimir-nabokov-talks-synesthesia on June 21, 2014. Mental Floss.

Blank on Blank. "David Foster Wallace on Ambition". 2013. Interview by Leonard Lopate, WNYC. 1996. Taken from https://www.youtube.com/watch?v=w5R8gduPZw4 on June 24, 2014.

Devey, Joseph. "Francis Bacon. The Advancement of Learning". 2014. Taken from http://oll.libertyfund.org/titles/1433 on June 21, 2014. Online Library of Liberty.

Godin, Seth. "The platform vs. the eyeballs". 2009. Taken from http://sethgodin.typepad.com/seths_blog/2009/09/the-platform-vs-the-eyeballs.html on June 21, 2014.

Gudgel, Andrew. "Commonplace Books – Old Wine in New Bottles". 2010. Taken from http://www.andrewgudgel.com/commonplace.htm on June 21, 2014.

Guildhall, Olivia. "The Science of Why We Live". Daily Telegraph. 2014.

Gilbert, Elizabeth, TED. "Your Elusive Creative Genius". 2009. Taken from http://www.ted.com/talks/elizabeth_gilbert_on_genius on June 21, 2014. TED.

Gray Matter. "Brain, Interrupted". 2013. Taken from http://www.nytimes.com/2013/05/05/opinion/sunday/a-focus-on-distraction.html?_r=1& on June 24, 2014. New York Times.

Hamilton, Jon. "Think You're Multitasking? Think Again". 2008. Taken from http://www.npr.org/templates/story/story.php?storyId=95256794 on June 24, 2014. NPR.

Holiday, Ryan. "How and Why To Keep a Commonplace Book". 2014. Taken from www.ryanholiday.net on June 21, 2014.

Isaac, Brad. "Jerry Seinfeld's Productivity Secret". 2007. Taken from http://lifehacker.com/281626/jerry-seinfelds-productivity-secret on June 21, 2014. Lifehacker.

Lavinsky, Dane. "Pareto Principle: How To Use It to Dramatically Grow Your Business". Forbes. 2014. Taken from http://www.forbes.com/sites/davelavin-sky/2014/01/20/pareto-principle-how-to-use-it-to-dramatically-grow-your-business/ on June 21, 2014. Forbes.

Lev Grossman. "Jonathan Franzen: Great American Novelist". Time Magazine. 2010. Taken from http://content.-time.com/time/magazine/article/0,9171,2010185,00.html on June 21, 2014. Time Magazine.

Mehta, Ravi. Zhu, Rui (Juliet) Zhu. Cheema, Amar. "Is Noise Always Bad? Exploring the Effects of Ambient Noise on Creative Cognition". 2012. Taken from http://www.js-tor.org/stable/10.1086/665048 on June 21, 2014. Chicago Journals.

Nielsen, Jakob. "How long do web users stay on webpages". 2011. Taken from http://www.nngroup.com/ar-ticles/how-long-do-users-stay-on-web-pages/ on June 21, 2014.

Plimpton, George. "Ernest Hemingway: The Art of Fiction No. 20. 1954". Taken from http://www.theparisre-view.org/interviews/4825/the-art-of-fiction-no-21-ernest-hemingway on June 21, 2014. The Paris Review.

No name. "Side Dish What Was Benjamin Franklin's Daily Routine?". 2013. Take from http://www.sidedishmag.-com/2013/07/me-and-benjamin.html on August 14, 2014. Side Dish.

The Air Force Departmental Publishing Office. "The Inverted Pyramid". Taken from http://commons.wikimedi-a.org/wiki/File:Inverted_pyramid_2.svg#mediaview-er/File:Inverted_pyramid_2.svg on June 21, 2014.

Watts, Robert. "J.K. Rowling Unmasked As Author of Acclaimed Detective Novel". 2013. Taken from http://www.telegraph.co.uk/culture/books/10178344/JK-Rowling-unmasked-as-author-of-acclaimed-detective-novel.html on June 21, 2014. The Telegraph.

Viatour, Luc. "Vitruvian man". 2014. Taken from www.Lucnix.be on June 21, 2014.

Writer's Relief Staff. "Famous Author Rejection Letters: True Stories Of Unbelievable Rejections". 2011. Taken from http://writersrelief.com/blog/2011/07/famous-author-rejection-letters/ on July 3, 2014. Writer's Relief.